The Living Corpse: A Drama In Six Acts And Twelve Tableaux...

Leo Tolstoy (graf)

THE LIVING CORPSE

THE LIVING CORPSE

A Drama in Six Acts and Twelve Tableaux

By

LEO N. TOLSTOI

Translated from the Russian

By Anna Monossowitch Evarts
(Mrs. E. M. Evarts)

NICHOLAS L. BROWN
NEW YORK 1919

TRANSLATOR'S NOTE

The drama "The Living Corpse" (Zhivoi Trup), was written in the year 1900, at Moscow, at Pirogov (the estate of Sergey Nikolaevich, Tolstoi's brother) and at Yashaya Polyana (Tolstoi's own estate.)

The following translation is made from the only authorized Russian edition based on the manuscripts in the possession of the late Count Tolstoi's daughter, A. L. Tolstaya.

WASHINGTON, D. C.

CHARACTERS

FEODOR VASILYEVICH PROTASOV (*Fedya*).

ELIZAVETA ANDREEVNA PROTASOVA, *his wife* (*Liza*).

MISHA, *their son.*

ANNA PAVLOVNA, LIZA'S *mother.*

VICTOR MICHAILOVICH KARENIN.

SASHA, *a young girl,* LIZA'S *sister.*

ANNA DMITRIEVNA KARENINA.

PRINCE SERGEY DMITRIEVICH ABREZKOV.

MASHA, *a young gipsy-girl.*

IVAN MAKAROVICH, *an old gipsy.* }
NASTASYA IVANOVNA, *an old gipsy-woman.* } MASHA'S *parents.*

AN OFFICER.

A COMPOSER.

FIRST GIPSY.

SECOND GIPSY.

A GIPSY-GIRL.

GIPSIES—*men and women.* (*The chorus.*)

A DOCTOR.

MICHAIL ALEKSANDROVICH AFREMOV.

Stachov. ⎫
Butkevich. ⎬ Fedya's *friends.*
Korotkov. ⎭

Ivan Petrovich Aleksandrov.

Voznesensky, Karenin's *secretary.*

Petushkov, *an artist.*

Artemyev.

Two Waiters.

An Innkeeper.

A Policeman.

The Prosecuting Attorney.

Meljnikov.

A Clerk.

A Young Lawyer.

The Sergeant-at-arms.

Petrushin, *a lawyer.*

A Lady.

An Officer.

A Court Attendant.

The Nurse at Protasov's.

Maid.

Afremov's Lackey.

Lackey at the Karenin's.

THE LIVING CORPSE

The Living Corpse

ACT I.

TABLEAU I.

The action takes place at St. Petersburg, at the home of Protasov. The scene represents a small dining-room.

SCENE I.

Anna Pavlovna; a plump, gray-haired lady, tightly-laced, is sitting alone at the tea-table.

SCENE II.

Anna Pavlovna; the nurse (enters with a tea-pot.)

NURSE: May I have a little water?

ANNA PAVLOVNA: Yes. How is little Misha?

NURSE: Restless, as might be expected. Nothing is worse than to have madame herself nurse the child. She has her troubles, you see, and the child suffers. What can the milk be like if the mother spends all night crying?

ANNA PAVLOVNA: It seems she has quieted down now.

NURSE: Quieted down indeed! It makes one sick to look at her! She was writing something and crying all along.

SCENE III.

Anna Pavlovna, nurse; and Sasha (enters).

SASHA: (*to the nurse*) Liza is looking for you.

NURSE: I'm going, I'm going. (*Nurse goes out.*)

SCENE IV.

Anna Pavlovna and Sasha.

ANNA PAVLOVNA: The nurse says she does not cease to cry. Can't she try and compose herself!

SASHA: You astonish me, mamma! She has left her husband, the father of her child, and you expect her to be composed.

ANNA PAVLOVNA: Not exactly composed. What's done is done. If I, her mother, not only consented to my daughter's leaving her husband, but was glad of it, it means that he deserves it. We should be glad, not sorry, that we have rid ourselves of such a horrid person,—such a jewel!

SASHA: Mamma, why do you speak like this? You know it isn't true. He is not horrid; on the contrary, he is a remarkable, a very remarkable man, in spite of his weaknesses.

ANNA PAVLOVNA: Precisely,—a remarkable man. As soon as he has any money in his hands—whether his own or that of other people—

SASHA: Mamma, he never took other people's money.

ANNA PAVLOVNA: Well, his wife's then.

SASHA: But he gave his entire fortune to his wife.

ANNA PAVLOVNA: Why shouldn't he give it to her, knowing well enough that he will squander it all before long, in any event.

SASHA: Whether he will squander it or not, I only know that a woman should not separate from her husband, and especially from one like Fedya.

ANNA PAVLOVNA: According to you she should have waited till he had squandered everything, and had brought his gipsy mistresses to the house.

SASHA: He has no mistresses.

ANNA PAVLOVNA: That's just where the trouble lies,—he has somehow bewitched you all. But not me, no indeed! I see through him, and he knows it. Were I in Liza's place, I would not have waited till now to throw him over; I'd have done it a year ago.

SASHA: How lightly you say all this.

ANNA PAVLOVNA: Oh, no! it's not easy for me, a mother, to see my daughter separated from her husband. Believe me, it is most painful. But just the same it's better than ruining her young life. I thank the Lord that she has made up her mind at last, and that it's all over.

SASHA: Perhaps it isn't.

ANNA PAVLOVNA: Oh, if he would only give her a divorce!

SASHA: What good would that do?

ANNA PAVLOVNA: Bear in mind that she is young, and may yet be happy.

SASHA: Oh, mamma! what terrible things you do say! Liza cannot learn to love another.

ANNA PAVLOVNA: Why not, if she were free? There are men a thousand times better than your

Fedya, and they would be only too happy to marry her.

SASHA: Mamma, you do wrong to talk that way. Of course, you are thinking of Victor Karenin; I know it.

ANNA PAVLOVNA: And why shouldn't I think of him? He has loved her for ten years, and she loves him in return.

SASHA: Loves him, but not as a husband. It's merely their friendship from childhood.

ANNA PAVLOVNA: We know those friendships! Let only nothing stand in the way!

SCENE V.

Anna Pavlovna and Sasha; maid enters.

ANNA PAVLOVNA: Well?

MAID: Madame sent the janitor with a note to Victor Michailovich.

ANNA PAVLOVNA: What madame?

MAID: Elizaveta Andreevna, the madame.

ANNA PAVLOVNA: Well, what of it?

MAID: Victor Michailovich sent word that he would soon be over.

ANNA PAVLOVNA: (*surprised*) We were just talking of him. Only I don't see why she sent for him. (*To Sasha.*) Perhaps you know?

SASHA: Perhaps I do, and perhaps I don't.

ANNA PAVLOVNA: Always secrets—

SASHA: Liza will be here soon. She will tell you.

ANNA PAVLOVNA: (*Shaking her head; to the maid*) The samovar needs to be warmed up. Take it, Dunyasha. (*maid takes the samovar, and goes out.*)

SCENE VI.

Anna Pavlovna and Sasha.

ANNA PAVLOVNA: (*to Sasha, who has risen to go*) It happened just as I foretold. She sent for him right away, of course.

SASHA: Perhaps she sent for him for an altogether different reason.

ANNA PAVLOVNA: Well, why then?

SASHA: At this moment Karenin means no more to her than the nurse Trifonovna.

ANNA PAVLOVNA: Very well, you'll see. I know her, let me tell you. She sent for him to console her.

SASHA: Oh, mamma, how little you know her if you can think—

ANNA PAVLOVNA: You'll see, all right. I'm glad, very glad.

SASHA: We'll see. (*turns and goes out.*)

SCENE VII.

Anna Pavlovna alone.

ANNA PAVLOVNA: (*shakes her head and mutters*) All right, let her. All right, let her. Well—

SCENE VIII.

Anna Pavlovna and maid (*enters.*)

MAID: Victor Michailovich is here.

ANNA PAVLOVNA: Very well. Show him in, and tell madame. (*maid goes out.*)

SCENE IX.

Anna Pavlovna and Victor Karenin.

VICTOR KARENIN: (*enters, shakes hands with Anna Pavlovna*) Elizaveta Andreevna sent me a note that I should come over. I was going to come to-night anyhow, so I'm very glad.—Is Elizaveta Andreevna well?

ANNA PAVLOVNA: Yes, but the baby is a little restless. She'll be here soon. (*sadly*) Yes, yes, hard times; you know everything, don't you?

VICTOR KARENIN: Yes. I was here, you know, the other day, when the letter from him came. But is it really definitely decided?

ANNA PAVLOVNA: I should say so! Why, of course! To go through all this once more would be terrible.

VICTOR KARENIN: Yes, this is truly a case of "measure ten times before cutting once." And to cut into the living is very hard.

ANNA PAVLOVNA: Naturally, it's hard. But, to be sure, their union was cut into long ago, so that to break it was not as hard as it seems. He understands very well that after all that has happened he dare not come back.

VICTOR KARENIN: Why so?

ANNA PAVLOVNA: How can you expect otherwise after all this nastiness, after he had sworn that it would not happen again, and that if it should, he would renounce his rights as a husband and give her full freedom?

VICTOR KARENIN: Yes, but what freedom is there for a woman bound in wedlock?

ANNA PAVLOVNA: Divorce! He promised to divorce her and we will insist upon it.

VICTOR KARENIN: But Elizaveta Andreevna loved him so much—

ANNA PAVLOVNA: Her love was subjected to such abuse that there is hardly a shred left of it. She had to put up with drunkenness, deceit, unfaithfulness. Could anyone possibly love such a husband?

VICTOR KARENIN: For love's sake one can do anything.

ANNA PAVLOVNA: You talk of love, but how can anyone love such a rag, who cannot be depended upon in any way? What do you think took place only lately?—(*looks around at the door and speaks hurriedly*) Their affairs had gone to pieces, everything had to be mortgaged, and there was nothing to pay with. Finally an uncle comes to the rescue with two thousand to pay off the interest. He takes this money and drops out of sight. As for the wife, she stays at home with a sick child, waiting, when at last a note comes from him—asking her to send him his linen and things!

VICTOR KARENIN: Yes, yes, I know.

SCENE X.

Anna Pavlovna, Karenin. Enter Liza and Sasha.

ANNA PAVLOVNA: You see, Victor Michailovich has come as you requested.

VICTOR KARENIN: Yes, I was detained a bit. (*shakes hands with the sisters.*)

LIZA: Thanks. I have a great favor to ask of you. And I have no one to turn to but you.

VICTOR KARENIN: I'll do everything I can.

LIZA: You know everything, of course—

VICTOR KARENIN: Yes, I know.

ANNA PAVLOVNA: I'll leave you. (*to Sasha*) Come along, let's leave them alone.

SCENE XI.

Liza and Karenin.

LIZA: Yes, he wrote me a letter that he considered it all ended. I (*restraining tears*) felt so offended, so—well, in a word, I consented to break off with him and answered that I accepted his decision.

VICTOR KARENIN: And now you regret it?

LIZA: Yes, I felt that it was bad on my part, that I couldn't do it. Anything is preferable to separating from him. Well, in a word, give him this letter. Please, Victor,—give him this letter, and tell—bring him back.

VICTOR KARENIN: (*surprised*) But how?

LIZA: Tell him that I ask him to forget everything and to return. I might simply have sent the letter. But I know him: his first impulse will, as usual, be a good one, but later, under someone's influence, he will change his mind and do something altogether different from his real intentions.

VICTOR KARENIN: I will do what I can.

LIZA: You are astonished that I should ask just you?

VICTOR KARENIN: No—well, to tell the truth, yes, I am astonished.

LIZA: But you are not angry?

VICTOR KARENIN: Can I be angry with you?

LIZA: I asked you because I knew that you loved him.

VICTOR KARENIN: Both him and you. You know it. I love not for myself, but for you. And I thank you for trusting me. I will do what I can.

LIZA: I know you will, and I will tell you all: I was just down at Afremov's to find out where he was. They told me he had gone to the gipsies.' And that's just what I am afraid of. It's that infatuation that I fear. I know that if he will not be restrained in time he will let himself be carried away. That's just what must be prevented. So you will go over?

VICTOR KARENIN: Of course, at once.

LIZA: Go over, find him and tell him that all is forgotten, that I am waiting for him.

VICTOR KARENIN: (*rises*) But where am I to look for him?

LIZA: He is at the gipsies'. I was there myself. I was at the door; I wanted to send the letter up, but I changed my mind and decided to ask you to do it for me. Here is the address. So tell him to come back, that nothing happened, that all's forgotten. Do it out of love for him and friendship for us.

VICTOR KARENIN: I will do all I can. (*bows and leaves.*)

SCENE XII.

Liza alone.

LIZA: I cannot, I cannot. Anything is better than—I cannot.

SCENE XIII.

Liza; Sasha (enters).

SASHA: Well, did you send it?

LIZA: (*nods yes.*)

SASHA: And he consented?

LIZA: Of course.

SASHA: Why him? I don't understand.

LIZA: Whom else?

SASHA: But you know that he is in love with you?

LIZA: All that was, and is no longer. But whom do you want me to ask, pray? Do you think he'll come back?

SASHA: I'm sure he will, because—

SCENE XIV.

Liza; Sasha; Anna Pavlovna. (*Sasha stops short.*)

ANNA PAVLOVNA: And where is Victor Michailovich?

LIZA: He's gone.

ANNA PAVLOVNA: Gone?

LIZA: I asked him to carry out my request.

ANNA PAVLONA: What request? Another secret?

LIZA: No secret at all. I simply asked him to give the letter personally to Fedya.

ANNA PAVLOVNA: To Fedya? To Fedor Vasilyevich?

LIZA: Yes, to Fedya.

ANNA PAVLOVNA: I thought it was all over between you two?

LIZA: I cannot part with him.

ANNA PAVLOVNA: What! Starting all over again?

LIZA: I wanted to, I tried to, but I couldn't. Anything you want rather than part with him.

ANNA PAVLOVNA: Well, do you mean to bring him back?

LIZA: Yes.

ANNA PAVLOVNA: Admit that nasty thing to the house again?

LIZA: Mamma, I ask you not to speak that way of my husband.

ANNA PAVLOVNA: He *was* your husband.

LIZA: No, he is my husband *now*.

ANNA PAVLOVNA: A squanderer, drunkard, libertine, and you cannot part with him?!

LIZA: Why do you torture me? I feel badly enough as it is, and you seem to torture me on purpose.

ANNA PAVLOVNA: I'm torturing you? Then I'll leave at once. I can't stand this.

LIZA: (*remains silent.*)

ANNA PAVLOVNA: I see that you want me to go, that I'm in your way. I cannot endure it. I don't understand any of your doings, any of those newfangled notions of yours. First you decide to separate from him, then you suddenly send for the man who is in love with you—

LIZA: Nothing of the kind.

ANNA PAVLOVNA: Karenin proposes to you—and you send him to fetch back your husband! And why? To arouse Karenin's jealousy?

LIZA: Mamma, what you say is terrible. Leave me!

ANNA PAVLOVNA: That's right—drive your mother out of the house and bring back your scamp of a husband. I won't be long in going, I tell you. Good-bye, then. The Lord be with you! Do as you please! (*goes out, slamming the door.*)

SCENE XV.

Liza and Sasha.

LIZA: (*drops into a chair.*) This is too much!

SASHA: Never mind! It'll turn out all right. We shall manage to pacify mamma.

SCENE XVI.

Liza; Sasha; Anna Pavlovna (*passes by.*)

ANNA PAVLOVNA: Dunyasha! My suit-case!

SASHA: Mamma, listen! (*follows her, and winks at her sister.*)

TABLEAU II.

SCENE I.

A room at the gipsies'. The chorus is singing "Kanavela." Fedya is lying on a couch, face down, without his coat. Afremov is astride of a chair, facing the leader of the chorus. An officer sits at a table on which stand champagne-bottles and glasses. At the same table a composer sits, taking down the melodies.

AFREMOV: Fedya, are you asleep?

FEDYA: Keep quiet! Now let's have "'Twas Not At Eventide."

GIPSY: Not just now, Feodor Vasilyevich. Now let Masha sing alone.

FEDYA: All right. But after that "'Twas Not At Eventide." (*lies down again.*)

OFFICER: "The Fatal Hour!"

GIPSY: Agreed?

AFREMOV: It'll do.

OFFICER: (*to the composer.*) Well, did you take it down?

COMPOSER: Impossible. It sounds different every time. And the scale is somehow altogether unusual. Look here (*to the gipsy girl, who is looking on*), how does this go? (*hums.*)

GIPSY GIRL: That's just right! That's fine!

FEDYA: (*rising.*) He won't take it down, and if he takes it down and sticks it into an opera he'll spoil it all. Well, Masha, let's have it, "The Hour," for all I care. Take the guitar. (*gets up, sits down in front of her, and gazes into her eyes.*)

MASHA: (*sings.*)

FEDYA: Bravo! Talk about Masha! Now let's have "'Twas Not At Eventide."

AFREMOV: No! Stop a moment! Sing mine first, a dirge.

OFFICER: Why a dirge?

AFREMOV: Why, because when I'll be dead—you understand, of course, that I shall die some time or other—the gipsies will come to my grave—you understand. That's what I'll demand of my wife in my last will. And they'll sing "A hundred leagues I wandered once," and I'll jump out of my grave—understand? (*to the composer*:) That's what you're to take down! Well, let's have it! (*the gipsies sing.*)

AFREMOV: Well, how's that? Now let's have "Come, brave lads." (*the gipsies sing.*)

AFREMOV: (*winks slyly*) *The gipsies smile and continue to sing; applause.*

AFREMOV: (*sits down. The singing comes to an end.*)

GIPSIES: Talk about Michail Aleksandrovich—a full fledged gipsy!

FEDYA: Now let's have "'Twas Not At Eventide." (*gipsies sing.*)

FEDYA: That's the way! That's it! Wonderful! And where does all that is expressed here happen? Ah, fine! Why can a man attain to such ecstasy, and not be able to sustain it?

COMPOSER: (*writing down*) Yes, it *is* very strange.

FEDYA: It's not strange; it's only truly beautiful.

AFREMOV: Now, let me try it (*takes the guitar and sits down near Katya.*)

COMPOSER: After all, it's very simple; it's all in the rhythm.

FEDYA: (*Motions disapproval, goes over to Masha and sits down on the sofa at her side*) Ah, Masha, Masha, how you stir my innermost being!

MASHA: Well, and what do I ask of you in return?

FEDYA: What? Money? (*takes some out of his trouser-pocket*) Well, here you are, take it.

MASHA: (*laughs, takes the money, and hides it in her bosom.*)

FEDYA: (*to the gipsies.*) How is one to understand it? To me she opens the gates of heaven, and all she cares for is the money she gets! You see, you don't for a moment understand what you are doing!

MASHA: Why don't I? I understand that whom I love, for him I try to sing my best.

FEDYA: And you love me?

MASHA: Plain enough I do.

FEDYA: Glorious! (*kisses her.*)

SCENE II.

The gipsies and the gipsy-girls go out. Three couples remain, Fedya with Masha; Afremov with Katya; the Officer with Gasha. The Composer continues writing. The gipsy runs his fingers over the strings of the guitar, playing a walse.

FEDYA: I'm married, you know. And as for you, the chorus doesn't one bit like what you're doing.

MASHA: The chorus can get along well enough without me, but a heart's a heart. Whom I love, I love. And whom I hate I hate.

FEDYA: Ah, wonderful! Are you happy?

MASHA: Of course I am. When the guests are the right sort, we, too, have a jolly time.

SCENE III.

A gipsy enters.

GIPSY: (*to Fedya*) A gentleman is asking for you.

FEDYA: Who is it?

GIPSY: I don't know. He's well dressed; a sable coat.

FEDYA: Somebody of importance? Well, call him in.

SCENE IV.

The same, without the gipsy.

AFREMOV: Who can be looking for you here?

FEDYA: The devil knows! Who has any business with me?

SCENE V.

The same; Karenin enters and looks around.

FEDYA: Ah, Victor! Didn't expect you, to be sure! Take off your things. What wind blew you here? Well, sit down. You'll hear "'Twas Not At Eventide."

VICTOR KARENIN: Je voudrais vous parler sans témoins.

FEDYA: What about?

VICTOR KARENIN: Je viens de chez vous. Votre femme m'a chargé de cette lettre, et puis——.

FEDYA: (*takes the letter, reads it, frowns, then smiling pleasantly.*) Listen, Karenin, you no doubt know what's in this letter?

VICTOR KARENIN: I know and wish to say——

FEDYA: Hold on, hold on. Please don't think that I am drunk, and that I'm not responsible for what I say. I am drunk, but in this matter I see everything clearly. Well, what were you instructed to say?

VICTOR KARENIN: I was instructed to find you and to tell you that—she—is waiting for you. She asks you to forget everything and to come back.

FEDYA: (*listens silently, looking in his eyes*) I don't understand, just the same, why it was you——?

VICTOR KARENIN: Elizaveta Andreevna sent for me and asked me to——

FEDYA: I see.

VICTOR KARENIN: But I ask you, not so much in your wife's name as in my own, to return home with me.

FEDYA: You're so much better than I am. What nonsense! It isn't very hard to be better than I am. I'm a good-for-nothing, and you're a very excellent person. And for this very reason I shall not change my decision. But that's not really the reason. I simply cannot and will not do it. And how could I?

VICTOR KARENIN: Let us go to my home now. I shall tell them that you will return, and to-morrow——

FEDYA: And to-morrow, what then? It will be all the same. I'll be I, and she'll be she (*goes to the table and takes a drink.*) A tooth should be pulled out at the first attempt. I told her, you know, that if I should break my word again, she should throw me over. I broke it: that ends it all.

VICTOR KARENIN: For you, but not for her.

FEDYA: Strange that you should be so anxious that our union should not be broken.

VICTOR KARENIN: (*is about to say something. Masha approaches.*)

FEDYA: (*interrupting him.*) Just hear how she sings "Through the fields a-sowing flax." Masha! (*the gipsies gather.*)

MASHA: (*in a whisper.*) I say, let's sing a toast to the stranger!

FEDYA: (*laughingly*) A toast to Victor Michailovich! (*the gipsies sing.*)

VICTOR KARENIN: (*listens in embarrassment, then asks:*) How much shall I give them?

FEDYA: Twenty-five will do.

VICTOR KARENIN: (*gives them the money.*)

FEDYA: Marvelous! Now let's have "Through the fields a-sowing flax." (*the gipsies sing.*)

FEDYA: (*looking around.*) Karenin has skipped! Well, to the deuce with him! (*the gipsies scatter.*)

SCENE VI.

Fedya: (*sitting down with Masha*) Do you know who that was?

Masha: I heard his name.

Fedya: He's an excellent chap. He came to take me home to my wife. She loves me, as big a fool as I am, and this is the way I behave!

Masha: Well, it's mean of you. You ought to go to her. You ought to pity her.

Fedya: You think I should? I think I shouldn't.

Masha: Naturally, if you don't love her, then you needn't. But love is a fine thing.

Fedya: How do you know?

Masha: I simply know; that's all.

Fedya: Well, kiss me. Boys! Once more "Through the fields," and then an end to it. (*the gipsies commence singing.*)

Fedya: Ah, glorious! If there were only no awakening——. Just to die like this——.

ACT II.

TABLEAU I.

Two weeks have passed since the first act. Liza's home. Karenin and Anna Pavlovna are sitting in the dining-room. Sasha enters.

SCENE I.

VICTOR KARENIN: Well?

SASHA: The doctor says the danger is over. Only we have to beware of a cold.

ANNA PAVLOVNA: And Liza is all worn out.

SASHA: He says it is false croup of a mild sort. (*pointing to a basket.*) What's this?

ANNA PAVLOVNA: Those are grapes that Victor brought.

VICTOR KARENIN: Won't you have some?

SASHA: Yes, she'll like them. She has become very nervous.

VICTOR KARENIN: Two nights without sleep, without food.

SASHA: (*smiling*) But you didn't sleep, either.

VICTOR KARENIN: I—that's another matter.

SCENE II.

The same. Enter Liza and the Doctor.

DOCTOR: (*impressively*) That's right. Change it every half hour if he's not asleep. If he's asleep, don't disturb him. You needn't paint his throat. The temperature of the room is to be kept constant.

LIZA: And if he has a choking spell again?

DOCTOR: He won't. But if he should—use the powders. In addition, give him one in the morning and one in the evening. I'll write out the prescription at once.

ANNA PAVLOVNA: Won't you have some tea, Doctor?

DOCTOR: No, thank you. My patients are waiting. (*sitting down at the table.*) (*Sasha brings him pen and ink.*)

LIZA: Are you sure it's not the croup?

DOCTOR: (*smiling*) Absolutely. (*writes.*)

VICTOR KARENIN: (*to Liza.*) Have some tea, then, or, still better, go and rest; just look at yourself and see what you look like!

LIZA: Now I'm myself again. Thank you. What a true friend you've been to me! (*pressing his hand.*) (*Sasha turns away in disgust.*)

LIZA: Thanks, dear friend. That's how a dear—

VICTOR KARENIN: What have I done? There's certainly nothing to thank me for.

LIZA: And who sat up nights? Who brought the specialist?

VICTOR KARENIN: I am amply rewarded by the fact that Misha is out of danger, and above all—by your appreciation.

LIZA: (*presses his hand again and laughs, showing him a coin that she held in her hand*) That's for the Doctor. But I never know how to give it to him.

VICTOR KARENIN: Neither do I.

LIZA: Think of giving money to a doctor! He has saved what is dearer to me than my life, and in return I offer him money. There's something so vulgar about it.

ANNA PAVLOVNA: Let me have it; I'll give it to him. I know how. It's very simple.

DOCTOR: (*rising and handing her the prescription.*) Dissolve one of these powders thoroughly in a tablespoonful of boiled water and—(*continues.*)

(*Karenin at the table, drinking tea. Anna Pavlovna and Sasha step into the foreground.*)

SASHA: I cannot endure their behaviour. She acts just as if she were in love with him.

ANNA PAVLOVNA: What's there so strange about that?

SASHA: It's disgusting.

DOCTOR: (*departs, bidding them all good-bye. Anna Pavlovna takes him to the door.*)

SCENE III.

Liza, Karenin, Sasha.

LIZA: (*to Karenin*) He's such a dear now. As soon as he felt better he began to smile and prattle. I'll go to him. And yet I don't want to leave you alone, either.

VICTOR KARENIN: But have some tea, have something to eat.

LIZA: I don't need anything now. I feel so well, now that all the torture is over. (*sobbing.*)

VICTOR KARENIN: There now, you see how weak you are!

LIZA: I am happy. Don't you want to look at him?

VICTOR KARENIN: Why, of course.

LIZA: Come along. (*they go out.*)

SCENE IV.

Anna Pavlovna (enters), Sasha.

ANNA PAVLOVNA: (*to Sasha.*) Why are you looking as solemn as an owl? I handed it to him very nicely, and he took it, too.

SASHA: It's sickening. She took him along with her into the nursery, as if he were her fiancé or her husband.

ANNA PAVLOVNA: What do you care? What are you fuming about? Perhaps you wanted to marry him?

SASHA: I! that poker? I would rather marry I don't know whom than him. I never even gave it a thought. I am only disgusted that Liza can get on such intimate terms with a stranger, after Fedya.

ANNA PAVLOVNA: A fine stranger indeed! A childhood friend!

SASHA: But I see by their smiles, their eyes, that they are in love with one another.

ANNA PAVLOVNA: What's there so strange about that? He took the child's illness so much to heart, showed so much sympathy and was so helpful. Naturally she's grateful; and, besides, why shouldn't she fall in love with Victor and marry him?

SASHA: That would be terrible, disgusting! Disgusting!

SCENE V.

Karenin and Liza enter.

VICTOR KARENIN: (*takes leave silently.*)

SASHA: (*goes out in anger.*)

SCENE VI.

Anna Pavlovna and Liza.

LIZA: (*to her mother.*) What's the matter with her?

ANNA PAVLOVNA: I really don't know.

LIZA: (*sighs silently.*)

TABLEAU II.

In Afremov's den. Glasses filled with wine. Guests.

SCENE I.

Afremov, Fedya, Stachov (shaggy, unkempt), Butkevich (smooth-faced), Korotkov (a hanger-on).

KOROTKOV: And I tell you she'll be left at the post! "La Belle Boas" can't be matched in Europe. What'll you bet?

STACHOV: Hold your horses, old boy! You know well enough that nobody believes a word of what you say, and that no one will take you up.

KOROTKOV: I tell you that your Kartush will be left at the post.

AFREMOV: Stop quarreling! Here's a way out of it! Ask Fedya; he'll tell you the truth.

FEDYA: Both horses are good. It all depends on the jockey.

STACHOV: Gusev is a rascal. You have to keep an eye on him.

KOROTKOV: (*shouting.*) It isn't so!

FEDYA: There now, just a moment; let me settle this for you. Who won the Derby?

KOROTKOV: He won it, but that doesn't signify anything. It was mere luck. If Krakus hadn't fallen sick——look——! (*lackey enters.*)

SCENE II.

The same, and the lackey.

AFREMOV: What is it?

LACKEY: There's a lady here—she wants to see Feodor Vasilyevich.

AFREMOV: What sort of a lady? A real one?

LACKEY: I can't tell, she looks like a real one.

AFREMOV: Fedya, a lady wants to see you.

FEDYA: (*frightened*) Who is it?

AFREMOV: He doesn't know.

LACKEY: I'll ask her into the parlor, anyhow.

FEDYA: Wait, I'll go and see. (*Fedya and the lackey go out.*)

SCENE III.

The same, without Fedya and the lackey.

KOROTKOV: Who can want him?—I suppose it's Masha.

STACHOV: Whom do you mean?

KOROTKOV: The gipsy-girl. She's in love with him. And she loves him as a cat loves.

STACHOV: She's a dear girl! And how she sings!

AFREMOV: Wonderfully! Tanyusha and she. Yesterday they sang, together with Peter——

STACHOV: There's a lucky dog for you!

AFREMOV: Because the women folks like him? God help them!

KOROTKOV: I can't stand those gipsy girls—there's nothing chic about them.

BUTKEVICH: Don't say that!

KOROTKOV: I would exchange them all for one French girl.

AFREMOV: You're a well-known judge of beauty. I think I'll go and see who it is—(*goes out.*)

SCENE IV.

The same, without Afremov.

STACHOV: If it's Masha, bring her in. We'll make her sing something. No, gipsies aren't what they used to be. There was one of them, Tanyusha—Ah!—There's no one like her!

BUTKEVICH: But I think they're all alike.

STACHOV: How can you say that, knowing that insipid ballads have taken the place of beautiful songs?

BUTKEVICH: There are some beautiful ballads, too.

KOROTKOV: What will you wager that I will have her sing something and you will not be able to tell whether it's a ballad or a song?

STACHOV: As usual, Korotkov is ready to bet.

SCENE V.

The same, and Afremov.

AFREMOV: (*enters*) Gentlemen, it is not Masha. And there's no other room but this one to receive the visitor in. Let's go into the billiard room. (*They all go out.*)

SCENE VI.

Enter Fedya and Sasha.

SASHA: (*confused*) Fedya, forgive me if I am embarrassing you; but for goodness' sake, listen to me. (*Her voice is trembling.*)

FEDYA: (*pacing the room*). (*Sasha has seated herself and looks at him.*)

SASHA: Fedya, come back home.

FEDYA: Listen, Sasha, I understand you very well. Sasha, my dear, I would have done the same in your place. I would have tried to somehow restore everything to its former state; but were you in my place, dear, sensitive little girl, as strange as it may sound—were you in my place, you would surely have done what I did, that is, you would have gone away, you would have refused to be in the way of another person's happiness.

SASHA: What do you mean by "in the way?" Do you think that Liza can live without you?

FEDYA: Ah, my dear, darling Sasha, she can, yes, she can, and she will still be happy, much happier than with me.

SASHA: Never!

FEDYA: That's what *you* imagine. (*holding her hand in his.*) But that isn't it. The main thing is that I can't, you see. You know how it is—take a piece of card-board and bend it this way and that, you may bend it a hundred times without breaking it, but bend it once more and you'll break it. That's the way it is with Liza and me. It hurts me too much to look her in the face, and she feels the same way, believe me.

SASHA: No, no!

FEDYA: You say no, but you know it's so.

SASHA: I only judge by myself. If I were in her place and you told me what you're telling me now—I should have felt perfectly miserable.

FEDYA: Yes, you would—(*silence; both are embarrassed.*)

SASHA: (*rising*) Must things really remain this way?

FEDYA: There's no help for it——

SASHA: Fedya, come back.

FEDYA: Thank you, dear Sasha. You will always hold a dear place in my memory. Well, good-bye, my dear. Let me kiss you. (*Kisses her forehead.*)

SASHA: (*Excited*) No, I won't say good-bye, I don't believe it, I can't believe it—Fedya!

FEDYA: Well, then listen. Only promise that you'll not repeat what I am about to tell you. Do you promise?

SASHA: Certainly.

FEDYA: Listen, then, Sasha. It is true I am her husband, the father of her child, but I am in the way. Wait, just a moment, don't contradict me. You think I am jealous? Not one bit. In the first place I have no right to be, and in the second place I have no cause. Victor Karenin is an old friend of hers and of mine too. And he loves her and she loves him.

SASHA: It's not true.

FEDYA: She loves as any honest, pure woman loves, who does not allow herself to love anybody but her husband. But she loves and is going to love him openly when this obstacle (*pointing to himself*) has been removed and I am removing it, and they will be happy. (*his voice trembles.*)

SASHA: Fedya, don't say that.

FEDYA: You know very well that it is true, and I shall rejoice in their happiness, and this is the best that I can do—I shall not return, I tell you, and I shall give them their freedom—and that's what you must tell them——. Don't, don't——. Good-bye! (*Kisses her on the forehead and opens the door.*)

SASHA: Fedya, I admire you!

FEDYA: Good-bye, good-bye——. (*Sasha goes out.*)

SCENE VII.

Fedya, alone.

FEDYA: Yes, yes—wonderful, excellent——. (*Rings.*)

SCENE VIII.

Fedya and the lackey.

FEDYA: Call your master.

SCENE IX.

FEDYA: It's true, it's true——.

SCENE X.

Afremov enters.

FEDYA: Let us go out.

AFREMOV: How did you manage things?

FEDYA: Fine! "She vowed and she promised." Excellently! Where is everybody?

AFREMOV: They're playing billiards upstairs.

FEDYA: Very well, let's go over there for a while.

ACT III.

TABLEAU I.

CHARACTERS.

Prince Abrezkov, a well-dressed bachelor of sixty, with a mustache, a dignified, serious-looking old soldier. Anna Dmitrievna Karenina (Victor's mother,) grande dame of fifty, who tries to appear youthful; she uses French expressions every now and then. Also Victor, Liza and the lackey.

(*Anna Dmitrievna's boudoir, simply yet sumptuously furnished, and full of souvenirs.*)

SCENE I.

Anna Dmitrievna and the lackey.

LACKEY: (*announces*) Prince Sergey Abrezkov.

ANNA DMITRIEVNA: Show him in. (*Turns around and tidies herself before the mirror.*)

SCENE II.

PRINCE ABREZKOV: (*entering*) J'espère que je ne force pas la consigne. (*Kissing her hand.*)

ANNA DMITRIEVNA: You know that vous êtes toujours le bienvenu, and just now especially so. Did you receive my note?

PRINCE ABREZKOV: Yes. And this is my answer.

ANNA DMITRIEVNA: Ah, my friend, I'm getting desperate. Il est ensorcelé, positivement ensorcelé. I never knew him to be so persistent, so obstinate, so heartless and indifferent to me. He's an altogether different person since that woman threw her husband over.

PRINCE ABREZKOV: Well, what is the matter? What does he want?

ANNA DMITRIEVNA: He wants to marry her, at any cost.

PRINCE ABREZKOV: And what about her husband?

ANNA DMITRIEVNA: He is willing to give her a divorce.

PRINCE ABREZKOV: Is that so!

ANNA DMITRIEVNA: And Victor is ready to plunge right into it, into all the mire, into all that mess of lawyers and testimony. Tout ça est dégoutant. Yet all that doesn't discourage him. I don't understand him. With all his sensitiveness and shyness, he—

PRINCE ABREZKOV:—is in love. Ah, if a man is really in love——

ANNA DMITRIEVNA: Yes, but why could love in our days be pure, uniting people by bonds of friendship that lasted through life? That's the kind of love I understand and value.

PRINCE ABREZKOV: Nowadays the new generation is not satisfied with such ideal relations. La possession de l'âme ne leur suffit pas. We cannot change that! But what about him?

ANNA DMITRIEVNA: What shall I tell you of him? He is as if under a spell. He is no longer his former self. You know—I went to see her. He begged me so much. I went over, but did not find her in, and left my card. Elle m'a fait demander si je ne pourrais la recevoir. So I'm expecting her soon (*looking at the clock*), at about two o'clock. I promised Victor to receive her, but just imagine the position I am in! I am not altogether myself; and by force of habit I sent for you, for I need your help.

PRINCE ABREZKOV: Thank you.

ANNA DMITRIEVNA: You must realize that this visit of hers will determine everything, Victor's whole life. I must either refuse to give my consent or—but how can I?

PRINCE ABREZKOV: Do you know her at all?

ANNA DMITRIEVNA: I have never seen her. But I'm afraid of her. A good woman could not possibly decide to leave her husband, especially since he is such a good man. He is a friend of Victor's, you know, and used to come to our house. He was charming. And even if he weren't. Quelsque soient les torts qu'il a en vis-à-vis d'elle, a woman should never leave her husband; she should bear her cross. One thing I cannot understand—and that is how Victor, with his principles, can think of marrying a divorced woman! How many times—why, only a short time ago, he had a hot argument with Spitzyn, in my presence, proving that divorce is contrary to the spirit of Christianity, and now he acts against his own convictions. Si elle a pu lui charmer a une telle point——. I am afraid of her. I called you, however, to get your advice,—and here I am doing all the talking! What is your opinion? Tell me! How do you feel about it? What do you think should be done? Did you speak to Victor?

PRINCE ABREZKOV: I did, and I think he really loves her; quite unawares, he has grown to love her deeply; this love has taken strong possession of him; you know how slow he is to make up his mind; so much the harder to make him change it once it is made up. What has once entered his heart will not be rooted out; he will love no one but her; and he will never be happy with another.

Anna Dmitrievna: And to think how ready Varya Kazantseva would have been to marry him! What a charming girl, and how she loves him!

Prince Abrezkov: (*smiling*) C'est compter sans son hôte. That is altogether out of the question now. And I think it would be best to give in and help him get married.

Anna Dmitrievna: To a divorced woman, so that he should meet his wife's husband? I don't understand how you can say that so calmly! Is that the sort of a woman a mother could wish to see her only son married to? And such a son as mine?

Prince Abrezkov: But what is to be done, dear friend? Of course, it would be better if he were to marry a girl whom you knew and loved; but if that is impossible——. And besides, what if he had married a gipsy, or heaven-knows-whom? And Liza Protasova—is a very nice, amiable woman. I know of her through my niece Nellie. She is a kind, gentle, loving, pure woman.

Anna Dmitrievna: A pure woman, who decides to throw her husband over?

Prince Abrezkov: This is not at all like you. You are unkind and unfair. Her husband is one of those men of whom it may be said that they are their own worst enemies. But he is a still greater enemy to his wife. He is a weak, depraved man, a drunkard. He has squandered his own fortune, and all of hers too,—and don't forget that she has a child. How can you blame a woman for leaving such a husband? Besides, it wasn't she who left him, but he who left her.

ANNA DMITRIEVNA: Oh, what filth, what mire! And I have to besmirch myself with it!

PRINCE ABREZKOV: And what does your religion teach you to do?

ANNA DMITRIEVNA: Yes, yes,—forgiveness. "As we forgive our debtors." Mais c'est plus fort que moi.

PRINCE ABREZKOV: How could she live with such a person, pray? Even if she didn't love anyone else, it was right for her to have done what she did, for the sake of her child. The husband himself, who is a kind and reasonable man, when he has his wits about him, advised her to do it——.

SCENE III.

Anna Dmitrievna, Prince Abrezkov; Victor enters. (Kisses his mother's hand, and greets Prince Abrezkov.)

VICTOR KARENIN: Mamma, I came to tell you just one thing. Elizaveta Andreevna will be here soon, and I ask and beg you to do only this: If you persist in refusing to give your consent to my marriage——

ANNA DMITRIEVNA: (*interrupting him*) Of course I shall persist in refusing to give my consent.

VICTOR KARENIN: (*continuing to talk, and frowning*) I have only one request to make of you: Don't mention your unwillingness to consent, and don't make up your mind too soon.

ANNA DMITRIEVNA: I don't think I shall care to discuss the matter. I, for one, shall certainly not broach the subject.

VICTOR KARENIN: Neither will she. I only wanted that you should get to know her.

ANNA DMITRIEVNA: There is one thing I cannot understand and that is, how you reconcile your desire to marry Madame Protasov, whose husband is living, with your religious principles that divorce is contrary to Christianity?

VICTOR KARENIN: Mamma, it's cruel of you! Do you mean to say that we are all so infallible that we cannot deviate from our opinions, when life is so complex? Mamma, why are you so cruel to me?

ANNA DMITRIEVNA: I love you, and I want to see you happy.

VICTOR KARENIN: (*to Prince Abrezkov*) Sergey Dmitrievich!

PRINCE ABREZKOV: Of course you want to see him happy, but we greyheads cannot understand the young people. It is especially hard for a mother who has become accustomed to her own idea of her son's happiness. All women are like that.

ANNA DMITRIEVNA: That's just it. Everybody is against me. Of course, you may do as you please, You're of age, vous êtes majeur——. But you will break my heart.

VICTOR KARENIN: This is so unlike you! This is worse than cruelty.

PRINCE ABREZKOV: (*to Victor*) Stop, Victor. Mamma always says more than she means.

ANNA DMITRIEVNA: I shall say what I feel and think, and I shall do so without hurting her feelings.

PRINCE ABREZKOV: We don't doubt it.

SCENE IV.

Anna Dmitrievna, Prince Abrezkov, Victor; the lackey (enters).

PRINCE ABREZKOV: Here she is.

VICTOR KARENIN: I shall go to receive her.

LACKEY: Elizaveta Andreevna Protasova.

VICTOR KARENIN: I'm going. Mamma, please—. (*leaves.*)

PRINCE ABREZKOV: (*also rising.*)

ANNA DMITRIEVNA: Show her in. (*to Prince Abrezkov*) No, remain here.

SCENE V.

Anna Dmitrievna and Prince Abrezkov.

PRINCE ABREZKOV: I thought you would feel more at ease en tête-a-tête.

ANNA DMITRIEVNA: No, I fear it. (*restless*) If I should want to remain tête-a-tête with her, I shall nod to you. Ça dépendra. Just now it would embarrass me to remain alone with her. I shall signal to you like this. (*makes a motion.*)

PRINCE ABREZKOV: I shall understand. I'm sure you will like her. Only be fair to her.

ANNA DMITRIEVNA: To think that you are all against me!

SCENE VI.

Anna Dmitrievna, Prince Abrezkov. Liza enters in a hat and afternoon-gown.

ANNA DMITRIEVNA: (*rising*) I was sorry not to find you in, but you have been kind enough to come over yourself.

LIZA: I never expected it. I am so grateful to you that you wanted to see me.

ANNA DMITRIEVNA: Have you met? (*pointing to Prince Abrezkov.*)

PRINCE ABREZKOV: Of course, I have had the honor of meeting Mme. Protasov. (*shaking hands, then sits down*) My niece Nellie often speaks of you.

LIZA: Yes, we were good friends. (*glancing timidly at Anna Dmitrievna*) And we are on friendly terms now too. (*to Anna Dmitrievna*) I never expected that you would want to see me.

ANNA DMITRIEVNA: I knew your husband well. He was friendly with Victor and used to call on us before he went to live in Tambov. I believe it was there that he married you?

LIZA: Yes, we were married there.

ANNA DMITRIEVNA: And, after that, when he came back to Moscow, he did not come to see us any more.

LIZA: Yes, he hardly went anywhere.

ANNA DMITRIEVNA: And he never arranged for us to meet. (*awkward silence.*)

PRINCE ABREZKOV: The last time I saw you was at the Demisov's, at a performance. It was very enjoyable. And you took part in it.

LIZA: No—Oh yes, I remember. I did take part. (*again silence*) Anna Dmitrievna forgive me, if what I'm going to say will hurt you, but I cannot, I don't know how to conceal my feelings. I came because Victor Michailovich said—because he—that is because you wanted to see me—but I would rather say it all—(*sobbing*)—my heart is heavy—and you are so kind.

PRINCE ABREZKOV: I think I'd better go.

Anna Dmitrievna: Yes, do.

Prince Abrezkov: Good-bye. (*takes leave of the two women and goes out.*)

SCENE VII.

Anna Dmitrievna and Liza.

Anna Dmitrievna: Listen. Liza—I don't know your full name, but it doesn't matter.

Liza: It's Liza Andreevna.

Anna Dmitrievna: Well, never mind—Liza. I am very sorry for you, I like you. But I love Victor. He is the only being in this world I love. I know his soul as I do my own. His is a proud soul. He was proud when a mere boy—proud not of his name and fortune, but of his purity, his moral standing; and he has preserved it. He is as innocent as a virgin.

Liza: I know it.

Anna Dmitrievna: He never loved any woman before. You are the first one. I won't say that I am not jealous of you. I am. But we mothers—your boy is still small, it's too early for you—we are preparing ourselves for it. I was preparing myself to yield him to a wife and not be jealous. But to yield him only to one as pure as himself.

Liza: I—do you mean that I——.

Anna Dmitrievna: Excuse me, I know it's not your fault, but you are unfortunate. I know him, however. At present he is ready to put up with everything and will do it; but he will suffer and never say a word. His wounded pride will suffer and he will be unhappy.

Liza: I was thinking of that myself.

Anna Dmitrievna: Liza, my dear, you are a

sensible, good woman. If you love him you long for his happiness more than for your own. And if that is the case, you don't want to tie him down and make him regret it, though he will never say so—never.

LIZA: I know he will not say it. I thought of it and asked myself that question. I thought it over and spoke to him about it. But what can I do if he says he doesn't want to live without me? I said: Let us be friends, don't dispose of your life, don't bind your pure life to my unfortunate one. But he wouldn't listen to me.

ANNA DMITRIEVNA: Yes, he doesn't want to listen now.

LIZA: Persuade him to leave me. I shall be satisfied. I love him for the sake of his happiness, not mine. Only stand by me, don't hate me. Let us seek his happiness together, in a spirit of love.

ANNA DMITRIEVNA: Yes, yes, I've learned to love you. (*kisses her; Liza weeps*) But this is terrible, just the same, terrible! If only he had fallen in love with you before you decided to get married——

LIZA: He says he did learn to love me then, but didn't want to stand in the way of his friend's happiness.

ANNA DMITRIEVNA: Oh, how pitiful it all is! But let us love each other, just the same, and the Lord will help us to see our way clear.

SCENE VIII.

Anna Dmitrievna, Liza and Victor.

VICTOR KARENIN: (*stepping forth*) Mamma, dear, I heard everything—I expected it! You have learned to love her, and everything will turn out well.

LIZA: What a pity that you heard everything—I would not have spoken—

ANNA DMITRIEVNA: I have come to no decision, just the same. I can only say this, that were it not for these aggravating circumstances, I would have been very much pleased. (*kisses her.*)

VICTOR KARENIN: Don't change your mind, please.

TABLEAU II

A modestly furnished room, a bed, writing desk and couch.

SCENE I.

Fedya, alone. A knock at the door. A woman's voice is heard from behind the door: "Why did you lock yourself in, Feodor Vasilyevich? Fedya, open the door!"

SCENE II.

Fedya and Masha.

FEDYA: (*rises and opens the door*) How nice of you to come! I was lonesome, very lonesome.

MASHA: Why didn't you come over to us? Drinking again? Oh, you! And you gave me your word!

FEDYA: You know, all my money is gone.

MASHA: Why did I learn to love you!

FEDYA: Masha!

MASHA: Yes, Masha, Masha. If you loved me you would have been divorced long ago. They were asking you for it, too. You say that you don't love her; yet you cling to her. Evidently you don't want——

FEDYA: You know well enough why I don't want to.

MASHA: That's all nonsense. They are right who say you are a will-o'-the-wisp!

FEDYA: What shall I say? To say that your words hurt me would be saying what you already know.

MASHA: Nothing hurts you——

FEDYA: You know yourself that there is only one joy in life for me—your love.

MASHA: My love is what it should be, but how about yours?

FEDYA: Well, I'm not going to assure you of it, there's no need of it; you know for yourself.

MASHA: Fedya, why do you torture me?

FEDYA: I should like to know who——

MASHA: (*weeping*) You are mean.

FEDYA: (*goes over, and embraces her*) Masha, what are you crying for? Stop it! One must live and not whimper. It doesn't become you at all, my little beauty!

MASHA: You love me?

FEDYA: Whom else should I love?

MASHA: Me alone? Well, read to me what you have written.

FEDYA: It will bore you.

MASHA: Since it's you who have written it, it must be all right.

Fedya: Well, listen. (*reads*) "In the late fall we agreed with our comrades to meet at the Murygin landing-place. That landing-place is on a rocky island abounding in wild fowl. It was a dull, warm, listless day. A fog——"

SCENE III.

Fedya and Masha. An old gipsy, Ivan Makarovich, and an old gipsy-woman, Nastasya Ivanovna, Masha's parents, enter.

Nastasya Ivanovna: (*approaching her daughter*) That's where you are, you runaway! Greetings to you, sir. (*to her daughter*) What are you doing to us? Tell me?

Ivan Makarovich: (*to Fedya*) It's not fair, sir. You're ruining the girl. It's not at all fair. You're acting mean.

Nastasya Ivanovna: Put on your shawl and get out at once! What do you mean by running away! What'll I tell the chorus? What do you mean by getting in with a beggar! What can he give you?

Masha: I'm not getting in with him. I love him and that's all. I'm not leaving the chorus. I'll sing, and as far——

Ivan Makarovich: Say another word and I'll pull your hair out, you good-for-nothing imp! Whose example are you following? Not your father's, nor your mother's, nor your aunt's. It's a shame, sir. We loved you; how often did we sing to you for nothing; we pitied you. And what did you do in return?

Nastasya Ivanovna: He has ruined our little girl, our own, our only one; he has dragged our jewel, our treasure into the mire—that's what he has done. You have no conscience.

FEDYA: Nastasya Ivanovna, you suspect me without any reason. Your daughter is like a sister to me. I guard her honor, and you will need have no fear. I love her—What else do you want me to do?

IVAN MAKAROVICH: It's strange you didn't love her when you had money. Then you might have paid the chorus about ten thousand roubles, say, and could have taken her in an honorable way. And now you have squandered everything and have taken her away by stealth. Shame on you, sir, shame on you!

MASHA: He didn't take me away, I came to him myself. And if you will take me back now, I'll go to him again. I love him, that's all! My love is stronger that all your bars—I don't want to return with you!

NASTASYA IVANOVNA: Well, Masha, darling, don't get angry. You did wrong; let's go now.

IVAN MAKAROVICH: Well, that'll do. Come! (*taking her by the hand*) Excuse us, sir. (*all three leave.*)

SCENE IV.

Fedya, Prince Abrezkov enters.

PRINCE ABREZKOV: Excuse me. I was an unintentional witness of an unpleasant scene.

FEDYA: Whom have I the honor of addressing? (*recognizing him*) Ah, Prince Sergey Dmitrievich. (*shaking hands.*)

PRINCE ABREZKOV: I said, an unintentional witness of an unpleasant scene. I wish I could have avoided hearing them. But since I have heard it all I consider it my duty to tell you so. I was directed to this room and had to wait at the entrance until those people left, all the more so since you could not have heard my knocking at the door on account of their loud talking.

FEDYA: Yes, yes, come right in, please. I thank you for having spoken of it, for it gives me a right to explain the meaning of this scene to you. It doesn't matter what you will think of me. But I wish to say that the reproaches which you heard them hurl at this girl—the gipsy singer—are unjust. The girl is as pure as a dove. And my relations to her are merely those of friendship. If, as may well be, they look to be romantic, that doesn't destroy the purity and honor of this girl. That's what I wanted to tell you. Now, what is it that you want of me? What can I do for you?

PRINCE ABREZKOV: In the first place, I——

FEDYA: Excuse me, Prince. My present position in society is such that my slight and remote acquaintance with you does not entitle me to a visit from you, unless you are here on some business. Well, what is it?

PRINCE ABREZKOV: I will not deny it; you guessed right. I am here on business. However, I beg you to believe that the change in your position can in no way influence my relation to you.

FEDYA: I am quite sure of that.

PRINCE ABREZKOV: I am here because I have been asked by the son of my old friend, Anna Dmitrievna Karenina, as well as by herself, to find out directly from you about your relations—I hope you will not mind my speaking of it—about your relations to your wife, Elizaveta Andreevna Protasova.

FEDYA: My relations to my wife, I may say to my former wife, are all ended.

PRINCE ABREZKOV: I thought so. And that's the only reason why I undertook this difficult commission.

FEDYA: They are ended, I hasten to state, not because of any fault of hers, but because of my fault, rather because of my unlimited faults. She, however, is as she has always been, a most unreproachable woman.

PRINCE ABREZKOV: So you see, Victor Karenin, and especially his mother, have asked me to find out from you just what your intentions are.

FEDYA: (*excited*) What intentions?—I have none. I give her complete freedom. More than that, I shall never disturb her peace. I know that she loves Victor Karenin. Well, let her. I consider him a great bore, but otherwise a very good, honest man, and I think she will be (as one usually puts it) happy with him. And—que le bon Dieu les bénisse! That's all.

PRINCE ABREZKOV: Yes, but we should——

FEDYA: (*interrupting*) And don't think that I am the least bit jealous. If I said of Victor that he was a bore, I take back that word. He is an excellent, honest, moral man, the very opposite of me. And he has loved her from his childhood. Perhaps she, too, loved him when she married me. That happens. The best love is the kind one is not conscious of. She always loved him, I think, but, as an honest woman, did not confess it even to herself. But that—a kind of shadow was thrown over our married life—However, why should I confess all this to you?

PRINCE ABREZKOV: Please do. Believe me that the most important thing in this visit is my desire to fully understand those relations. I understand you.

I understand that this shadow, as you so well expressed it, must have been—

FEDYA: It certainly was, and that's perhaps the reason why I could find no satisfaction in the sort of married life she was offering me. I was longing for something else, and so let myself be carried away. This, however, may seem as if I were trying to justify myself. I do not wish to justify myself, nor is it possible for me to do so. I *was*, I purposely say *was*, a bad husband, I *was*, because now I consider myself no longer her husband. I consider her perfectly free. So there you have an answer to your commission.

PRINCE ABREZKOV: But you know Victor's family and himself. His relations to Elizaveta Andreevna always were and continue to be most respectful and formal. He helped her when she was in trouble.

FEDYA: Yes, I encouraged their intimacy by my loose life. What can be done? It had to be that way.

PRINCE ABREZKOV: You know his and his family's strict orthodox principles. I don't share them; I look upon those matters from a broader point of view. But I respect and understand them. I understand that for him, and especially for his mother, any union with a woman, without the sanction of the church, is out of the question.

FEDYA: Yes, I know how stup—how straight-laced and conservative he is in this respect. But what do they want? A divorce? I told them long ago that I was willing to give it, but to have to take upon myself the whole guilt, and to face all the lies connected with it, is very hard.

PRINCE ABREZKOV: I fully understand you and agree with you. But what is to be done? I think it could be arranged——. However, you are right. It's terrible, and I sympathize with you.

FEDYA: (*pressing his hands*) Thanks, dear Prince. I always considered you a good, honest man. Now tell me, how am I to act? What shall I do? Just realize the position I am in. I don't try to grow better. I'm a good-for-nothing. But there are things which I cannot do calmly. I cannot tell a lie calmly.

PRINCE ABREZKOV: I don't understand you, after all. How can you, an able, sensible man, so susceptible to everything that's good—how can you let yourself be carried away, how can you so forget what you owe to yourself? How did you reach this stage, how did you ruin your life?

FEDYA: (*restraining tears of emotion*) I have been leading this loose life for the last ten years, and this is the first time that a man in your station has expressed any sympathy for me. I have had the sympathy of my comrades, of sports, of women, but of a sensible, good man like you— Thank you! How did I fall so low? Blame it upon wine, first of all. It isn't for its taste that I like it, but whatever I do, I always feel that I am not doing what I should, and I feel ashamed of myself. Just now I am talking to you, and I feel ashamed of myself. And when it comes to being a leader, holding a position in a bank—I'm so embarrassed, so ashamed of myself—and it's only when you take a drink that you cease feeling ashamed of anything. And music—not operas and Beethoven, but gipsy music—it's inspiring, it fills you with such energy! And don't forget those lovely black eyes and smiles. Yet the more entrancing it is, the more ashamed of oneself one feels afterwards.

PRINCE ABREZKOV: Well, and how about work?

FEDYA: I tried it. Nothing would do. I was

dissatisfied with everything. However, why talk about myself? Thank you.

PRINCE ABREZKOV: What shall I say, then?

FEDYA: Say that I will do what they want me to. They want to get married, don't they—they want nothing to prevent them from marrying?

PRINCE ABREZKOV: Of course.

FEDYA: I will do it, tell them; I will surely do it.

PRINCE ABREZKOV: When?

FEDYA: Wait a while. Well, in two weeks, let us say. Is that all right?

PRINCE ABREZKOV: (*rising*) So I may tell them that?

FEDYA: You may. Good-bye, Prince; thank you again.

(*Prince Abrezkov goes out.*)

SCENE V.

Fedya, alone.

FEDYA: (*sits for a long time, smiling silently*) Good, very good. That's just it; that's it, that's it! Excellent!

ACT IV

TABLEAU I

At an inn. A private room. The waiter ushers in Fedya and Ivan Petrovich Aleksandrov.

SCENE I.

Fedya, the waiter, and Ivan Petrovich (at the door.)

WAITER: Right here, please. No one will disturb you here, and I shall bring you some paper right away.

IVAN PETROVICH: Protasov, I want to come in.

FEDYA: (*seriously*) Come in if you want to, but I'm busy and—— Come in.

IVAN PETROVICH: You are going to reply to their demands? I'll tell you how to do it. I wouldn't go about it that way. I always talk frankly and act determinately.

FEDYA: (*to the waiter*) A bottle of champagne. (*waiter goes out.*)

SCENE II.

Fedya and Ivan Petrovich. (Fedya takes out a revolver and puts it down.)

FEDYA: Wait a while.

IVAN PETROVICH: What? You want to shoot yourself? Go ahead, go ahead! I understand you. They want to humiliate you, and you'll show them who you are. You'll kill yourself with a revolver, and them with your magnanimity. I understand you. I understand everything, because I am a genius.

FEDYA: Of course, of course. Only—(*waiter enters with paper and ink.*)

SCENE III.

Fedya, Ivan Petrovich, and the waiter.

FEDYA: (*covers the revolver with a napkin*) Open the bottle. Let's drink. (*They drink.*) (*Fedya writes*) Wait a while.

IVAN PETROVICH: Here's to your—long journey! I am above all that, you see. I will not attempt to stop you. A genius is equally indifferent to life and death. I am dead during life, and live after death. You will kill yourself, so that those two people should pity you. And I—I shall kill myself, so that the whole world should realize what it has lost. I shall not hesitate or reflect, either. I take it (*grasps the revolver*) a moment—and it's all over. But the time has not yet come for it. (*Puts back the revolver*) Nor need I leave any notes behind; they ought to understand for themselves. Ah, you——

FEDYA: Stop a moment!

IVAN PETROVICH: How pitiful people are! They hurry and scurry, and yet don't understand, don't comprehend anything. I'm not talking to you. I am just expressing my thoughts. And what does humanity need? Very little; only to learn to appreciate its geniuses. But it has always executed, persecuted, and tortured them. No—I will not be your toy! I shall expose you! No-o-o-o. Hypocrites!

FEDYA: (*has finished writing, reads while drinking*) Go away, please.

IVAN PETROVICH: Go away? Well, good-bye. I will not attempt to stop you. I'll do the same. But it's yet too early. I only want to tell you——

FEDYA: All right; you'll tell me a little later, but now listen to this, my friend. Please give this to the landlord (*handing him some money*), and ask him for a letter and a package in my name. Please, do.

IVAN PETROVICH: Very well. So you'll wait for me? I have something important to tell you, something that you will have no chance to hear, not only in this world, but not even in the next one, at least not until I get there. Am I to give him all this?

FEDYA: As much as I owe him. (*Ivan Petrovich goes out.*)

SCENE IV.

Fedya, alone.

FEDYA: (*breathes a sigh of relief, closes the door after Ivan Petrovich, takes the revolver, raises it, puts it to his temple, shivers and lets it down carefully. Roars.*)

FEDYA: No, I cannot, cannot, cannot! (*knock at the door*) Who is it? (*Masha's voice behind the door. I!*)

FEDYA: Who is it? Ah, Masha! (*opens the door.*)

SCENE V.

Fedya and Masha.

MASHA: I was at your room, at Popov's, at Afremov's, and finally decided that you must be here. (*sees the revolver*) That's nice! There's a fool for you! A fool indeed! Did you really mean to do it?

FEDYA: No, I could not.

MASHA: And what of me? You heartless man! You did not pity me? Ah, Fedor Vasilyevich, it's a sin, a sin! For my love——

FEDYA: I wished to set them free, I promised. And I cannot lie.

MASHA: And what of me?

FEDYA: I would have broken your fetters, too. Or do you prefer to suffer with me?

MASHA: Of course I do. I cannot live without you.

FEDYA: What sort of a life is this? You would have wept some and then you would have gone on living.

MASHA: Indeed, I would not have wept at all! To the deuce with you, if you have no pity for me (*weeps.*)

FEDYA: Masha, my love, I wanted to improve matters.

MASHA: Yes, for yourself.

FEDYA: (*smiling*) How would I have been better off, if I had killed myself?

MASHA: Of course you would have been better off. But what do you need? Tell me.

FEDYA: What do you mean? I need many things.

MASHA: Well, what, what?

FEDYA: I need, first of all, to keep my promise.

That's the first thing, and that's enough. I cannot lie and do all those nasty things that are necessary for a divorce.

MASHA: I'll admit they are nasty. I myself—

FEDYA: Then I need to set them free, both my wife and him. Why not? They are nice people. Why should they suffer? That's the next thing.

MASHA: Well, I cannot see much good in her, if she threw you over.

FEDYA: She didn't throw me over—I did it all.

MASHA: Very well, very well. It's all your fault. She's an angel. What's next?

FEDYA: The next thing is that you are a dear, good little girl,—I love you; and if I remain alive I shall ruin you.

MASHA: You needn't trouble yourself about that, let me tell you. Leave it to me to decide what will ruin me.

FEDYA: (*sighs*) And the main thing, the main thing is: What does my life amount to? Don't I see that I am lost, a mere good-for-nothing? I am a burden to myself and to everybody else, as your father said. I'm a good-for-nothing!

MASHA: Just listen to that nonsense! You can't shake me off! I shall cling to you, that's all! As for your leading a bad life and drinking—Well, you're a man. Drop it! That's all!

FEDYA: That's easily said.

MASHA: Just do it.

FEDYA: There, when I look at you, it seems as if I could do anything.

MASHA: And you will do it. You will do everything. (*notices the letter*) What's that? You wrote to them? What did you write?

FEDYA: What did I write? (*takes the letter and wants to tear it up*) Now I don't need it any more.

Masha: (*snatches the letter out of his hand*) Did you write you killed yourself? Yes? You didn't mention the revolver? Did you mention the word killed?

Fedya: Yes, I said I would no longer exist.

Masha: Let me have it, let me, let me! Have you ever read "What's To Be Done?"

Fedya: I think I have.

Masha: It's a tedious novel, but one thing about it is very, very good. He, what's his name?—Rachmanov—went to work and pretended to have been drowned. So you—you don't know how to swim, do you?

Fedya: No.

Masha: That's just it. Let me have your clothes; everything, your wallet, too.

Fedya: What do you mean?

Masha: Wait, wait, just wait! Let us go home. You'll change your clothes there.

Fedya: But that's deceit!

Masha: Never mind! You see, you went in bathing, your clothes were left on the shore. In the pocket will be found your wallet and this letter.

Fedya: Well, and what then?

Masha: Then? Then we'll go away from here and live happily forever after.

SCENE VI.

Fedya, Masha; Ivan Petrovich enters.

Ivan Petrovich: What do you think of that! Where's the revolver? I'll take it.

Masha: Take it. Do. We're going away.

TABLEAU II

A drawing-room at Mme. Protasov's.

SCENE I.

Karenin, Liza.

VICTOR KARENIN: He promised it so definitely that I'm sure he'll keep his word.

LIZA: I'm ashamed to admit it, but I must say that after what I have found out about that gipsy-girl, I feel entirely free. Don't think it's jealousy. It's not that, it's rather a feeling of liberation that I have. How shall I make you understand it? What was torturing me above everything else was that I felt I was loving two men at once. And that means that I am an immoral woman.

VICTOR KARENIN: You an immoral woman?

LIZA: But the moment I found out that he had dealings with another woman, which means that he doesn't need me, I considered myself free, and felt that I could, without lying, tell you that I loved you. Now my soul is at ease, and I am troubled only by the condition I am in, by that divorce. All that is so trying, especially the anticipation of it.

VICTOR KARENIN: It will be over soon, very soon. In addition to Fedya's promise, I asked the secretary to go to him with the application and not to leave before he will have signed it. If I didn't know him as well as I do, I would have thought he was delaying on purpose.

LIZA: On purpose? No, it's always that same weakness and honesty of his. He will not say what isn't true. It was in vain you sent him the money.

VICTOR KARENIN: Why not? It might have been a cause of delay.

LIZA: No, it doesn't seem quite right to have sent him money.

VICTOR KARENIN: Well, he can now afford to be a little less punctilious.

LIZA: What egoists we have become!

VICTOR KARENIN: Yes, I admit it. But you have no one to blame but yourself. I am very happy now, after all that waiting, that hopelessness; and happiness makes us selfish. It's all your fault.

LIZA: You think you are the only one who feels that way. I feel just the way you do. I am floating on the wings of happiness. Everything has come our way. Mika is getting better, your mother loves me, and you love me, and, what is most important, I love you!

VICTOR KARENIN: You do? Without regrets? With no return?

LIZA: From that day on everything within me suddenly took a new turn.

VICTOR KARENIN: And it can never be different again?

LIZA: Never. I only wish it should be as final with you as it is with me.

SCENE II.

Karenin, Liza, the nurse with the baby. (*The nurse enters with the baby. The boy goes to his mother, who takes him on her lap.*)

VICTOR KARENIN: What unfortunate people we are!

LIZA: What makes you say that? (*kisses the child.*)

VICTOR KARENIN: When you were married and when, after your return from abroad, I found it out and felt that I had lost you, I was unhappy, and I was glad to learn that you remembered me. That was enough for me. Then, when we resumed our friendly relations and I felt that you cared for me, that there was in our friendship a tiny spark of something more than mere friendship, I began to feel almost happy. I was only tortured by the fear that I was not honest towards Fedya. I was always so firmly convinced, however, of the impossibility of anything but the purest friendship in my relations to my friend's wife—and I knew you too—that it didn't trouble me very long, and I was satisfied. Then, when Fedya began to torment you and I felt that I was a comfort to you, and that you feared my friendship, I was altogether happy, and a certain indefinite hope sprang up within me. Later on, when he became quite unbearable, you decided to leave him, and when I told you everything for the first time, and you didn't say no, but turned away from me in tears, my happiness was complete. If anyone would have asked me then what else I wanted, I should have answered: "Nothing." Then we saw a chance of uniting our lives, mamma learned to love you, realization became possible; you told me you had always loved me and loved me now; then you told me, as you did just now, that he did not exist for you, that you loved only me—what else could one ask, what else could I wish for? But no, at present I am tormented by the past. I wish that past had never been, that there was nothing to remind us of it.

LIZA: (*reproachfully*) Victor!

VICTOR KARENIN: Liza, forgive me. I say this because I don't want to have any thoughts concerning you hidden from you. All this I said on purpose to show you how mean I was, and since I know that I have reached the limit, I have to struggle with myself and conquer myself. And I have conquered. I love him.

LIZA: That's what you ought to do. I did all I could. I didn't really do it, but in my heart everything was transformed into just what you could have wished for; everything has disappeared from it, except you.

VICTOR KARENIN: Everything?

LIZA: Everything, everything! I would not say so if it were not true.

SCENE III.

Karenin, Liza, nurse with the baby, and lackey.

LACKEY: Mr. Voznesensky.

VICTOR KARENIN: There he is, with a reply from Fedya.

LIZA: (*to Karenin*) Let him come in here.

VICTOR KARENIN: (*rises and goes to the door*) There he is with an answer.

LIZA: (*gives the child to the nurse; nurse and child leave*) Is it really all coming to an end, Victor?

SCENE IV.

Karenin, Liza and Voznesensky (enters.)

VICTOR KARENIN: Well?

VOZNESENSKY: He was not in.

VICTOR KARENIN: What do you mean? And he has not signed the application?

VOZNESENSKY: The application is not signed, but he left a letter addressed to you and Elizaveta Andreevna. (*takes a letter out of his pocket*) I reached the house; they told me he was at the inn. I went there. Then Fedor Vasilyevich told me to come back in an hour when I would find the answer ready. I came, and——

VICTOR KARENIN: Another delay? New excuses? No, that's simply base! How low he has fallen!

LIZA: But read, see what the letter says!

VICTOR KARENIN: (*opens the letter.*)

VOZNESENSKY: You don't need me?

VICTOR KARENIN: Yes,—no, good-bye. Thank you. (*stops reading with a look of astonishment on his face. Voznesensky goes out.*)

SCENE V.

Karenin and Liza.

LIZA: What is it, what?

VICTOR KARENIN: It's terrible!

LIZA: (*seizes the letter*) Read!

VICTOR KARENIN: (*reads*) "Liza and Victor, I am addressing this to you both. I will not lie by calling you dear or beloved. I cannot overcome a certain feeling of bitterness and reproach—reproach towards myself, which is none the less tormenting—when I think of you, your love, your happiness. I know everything. I know that although I am the husband, circumstances have brought it about that I was really in your way. C'est moi, qui suis l'intrus. Just the same, I cannot refrain from a feeling of resentment and coolness towards you. Theoretically I love you both, especially Liza, my dear Liza, but in reality my feelings are more than cool. I know I'm in the wrong, but I cannot change myself.

LIZA: How could he——

VICTOR KARENIN: (*continues to read*) "But to the point! This very feeling that is dividing me against myself forces me to carry out your wish in a manner different from the one you wished for. To lie, to play base comedy by bribing the officials, to face all that meanness is disgusting to me. As mean as I may be, my meanness is of a different kind, and I can take no part in this baseness, I simply *cannot* do it. Another solution which presents itself to me is much simpler. You have to get married to be happy. I am in the way, therefore I have to destroy myself.

LIZA: (*grasps Karenin by the hand*) Victor!

VICTOR KARENIN: (*reads on*)—have to destroy myself. And so I am destroying myself. When you receive this letter I shall be no more.

P. S. I am very sorry you sent me that money for the trial. It was indelicate and not at all like you. But what's to be done? I was mistaken so many times, so you, too, may be mistaken once. The money will be returned to you. My solution is more brief, cheaper and surer. I beg one thing of you, don't be angry with me, and hold me in kind memory. One thing more. There's a watchmaker, Evgenyev; can't you do something for him to put him on his feet? He is a weak but kind-hearted man. Good-bye. Fedya."

LIZA: He has killed himself! But——

VICTOR KARENIN: (*rings, runs into the hall*) Call back Voznesensky!

LIZA: I knew it, I knew it! Fedya, dear Fedya!

VICTOR KARENIN: Liza!

LIZA: It's not true, no, it isn't true that I didn't love him; that I don't love him now! I love no one but him! I do! And I ruined him! Leave me! (*Voznesensky enters.*)

SCENE VI.

Karenin, Liza and Voznesensky.

VICTOR KARENIN: Where is Feodor Vasilyevich? What did they tell you?

VOZNESENSKY: They said he went out in the morning, left his letter and didn't return.

VICTOR KARENIN: That must be investigated. Liza, I leave you.

LIZA: Forgive me, but I too cannot lie. Leave me now. Go, find out——

ACT V

TABLEAU I

A dirty room in an inn. Around the tables sit several people who are drinking tea and whisky. In the foreground is a small table at which Fedya is seated, wasted and tattered; with him is Petushkov, a gentle, attentive person, with long hair, of a clerical aspect. Both are a little tipsy.

SCENE I.

Fedya and Petushkov.

PETUSHKOV: I understand, I understand. There's real love for you! Well, and what happened?

FEDYA: You see, if these feelings had manifested themselves in a girl of our circle, if one of them had sacrificed everything for the man she loved—but she was a gipsy, brought up on greed, and yet capable of such pure, self-sacrificing love. She gave up everything and asked nothing in return. An exceptional contrast that is especially remarkable.

PETUSHKOV: Yes, that is what we call tone-value in painting. One may use a bright red only when there is green all around. But that's not it. I understand, I do.

Fedya: Yes, and I believe the one good act I have to my credit is not to have taken advantage of her love. And do you know why?

Petushkov: Out of pity?

Fedya: Oh, no. I did not have any pity for her. I always felt enraptured in her presence, and when she sang, oh, how she sang! She is probably singing now, too. I always used to look up to her. I did not ruin her simply because I loved her, loved her truly. And now all that remains a wonderfully glorious memory with me. (*drinks.*)

Petushkov: That's it. I understand, I do. It was ideal.

Fedya: Let me tell you: I have had infatuations, and once I fell in love with a great lady, a beauty; I was in love with her in a mean, dog-like way; she made an appointment with me and I didn't appear, because I thought it mean towards her husband; and to this very day, strange as it may seem, whenever I think of it, I try to feel pleased and to praise myself for having acted honorably; but instead of that, I simply regret it, as one regrets his sins. But when it comes to Masha, I feel just the opposite way. I'm always glad, very glad, that I didn't in any way pollute that feeling of mine for her. I may fall still lower, I may perish altogether, I may sell all I have, become filthy and diseased, but this jewel, no, not jewel, but ray of sunshine, yes—will always be within me, always with me.

Petushkov: I understand. I understand. But where is she now?

Fedya: I don't know, and I don't care. That all belongs to another life, and I don't want to mingle it with this one.

(*From the table in the rear a woman's screams are heard. The innkeeper and a policeman go over;*

several people are led away. Fedya and Petushkov look on, listening silently.)

PETUSHKOV: (*after quiet has been restored*) Yes, you have led a remarkable life.

FEDYA: No, it's a very simple one. In our circle, the one in which I was born, we have but three courses to choose from—and no more than three. One is to enter the service, to make money, to increase the nastiness in the midst of which we live. That disgusted me; perhaps I didn't know how to do it, but the main thing was,—that it was disgusting to me. The second choice is to destroy that nastiness; but for that one has to be a hero, and I'm not a hero. There remains the third choice; to forget oneself,—to drink, frolic, sing; which is what I did, and this is the state I have sung myself into. (*drinks.*)

PETUSHKOV: Well, what about your home life? I could be happy if I had a wife. My wife is the one who ruined me.

FEDYA: Home life? Yes. My wife was an ideal woman. She is still alive. But what shall I say? There was no spice to her. You know how necessary spice is to give taste to the pudding. You see, there was no sparkle to our life. I had to forget myself, but without sparkle you cannot do it. Then I began to be mean; and you know, to be sure, that we love people for the good we do them, and we dislike them for the evil we do them. And I caused her evil. Yet she seemed to love me.

PETUSHKOV: Why do you say "seemed?"

FEDYA: I say that, because she never had the faculty of getting right into the depth of my soul, as Masha did. But that is what I wanted to tell you. She was with child, nursing, and I would disappear and come home drunk. Naturally, for that reason I loved her still less. Yes, yes (*becomes enraptured*), it just occurred to me; the reason I love Masha is because I treated her with kindness and not with harshness. That's why I love her. But the other one I tormented, and for that reason—it isn't exactly that I didn't love her—well, I simply didn't love her. I was jealous, it's true, but that too has passed away.

SCENE II.

Fedya, Petushkov, and Artemyev.

Artemyev approaches; wears a uniform cap, his moustache is dyed, his ancient clothes are fixed up.

ARTEMYEV: Good appetite to you! (*bows to Fedya*) I see you have become acquainted with the artist.

FEDYA: (*cooly*) Yes, we're acquainted.

ARTEMYEV: (*to Petushkov*) Well, have you finished the portrait?

PETUSHKOV: No, it didn't come out well.

ARTEMYEV: (*sits down*) I hope I'm not intruding. (*Fedya and Petushkov keep silent.*)

PETUSHKOV: Feodor Vasilyevich was telling me about his life.

ARTEMYEV: Secrets? Don't let me interrupt you; go right on—I certainly don't need you. Pigs!

(*Goes to the next table and orders beer. Through all that follows he listens to the conversation between Fedya and Petushkov, leaning over towards them.*)

FEDYA: I don't like that fellow.

PETUSHKOV: He took offense at us.

FEDYA: Well, that can't be helped. I can't endure him. He's the sort of man in whose presence

I am without words. With you, you see, I feel at ease, at home. What was it I was talking about?

PETUSHKOV: You were saying you had been jealous. Well, and how did you happen to part with your wife?

FEDYA: Ah! (*becomes thoughtful*) That is a remarkable story. My wife is married——

PETUSHKOV: How's that? Did you divorce her?

FEDYA: No! (*smiling*) She was widowed.

PETUSHKOV: What do you mean?

FEDYA: I mean what I say; she was widowed. You see, I don't exist.

PETUSHKOV: How can that be?

FEDYA: I don't exist. I'm a corpse. Yes. (*Artemyev leans over, listening intently*) Well, to you I suppose I may tell it. It is a matter of the remote past, and you don't even know my real name. It was like this: When I had finished tormenting my wife, had squandered everything I could lay my hands on, and became unendurable, a protector of hers appeared on the scene. Don't think there was anything nasty or bad about it—no, he was a friend of mine, a good, a very good man, only the very opposite of me in every respect, and since there's much more of the bad than of the good in me, he always was and is now a very good man; honest, firm, temperate, in a word, thoroughly virtuous. He knew my wife from her very childhood, he had loved her, and when she married me, he resigned himself to his fate. But later, when I grew abusive, when I began to torment her, he began to call on us more often. I myself wished him to do it, and they fell in love with each other; I had, however, by that time lost all self-respect, and, of my own accord, deserted my wife. Besides, there was Masha. I myself suggested to them that they should get married. They didn't want to, but I became more and more unbearable, and the end of it all was——

PETUSHKOV: The usual one.

FEDYA: No, I am sure that their relations have always been pure. He is a religious person, he would consider marriage without the sanction of the church a sin. Well, they began to demand a divorce and to urge me to consent to it. It meant that I should take the guilt upon myself, that I should do all the lying—and that I couldn't do. Will you believe me, I would have found it easier to commit suicide than to lie. And I was all ready to put an end to everything, but at the last moment a kind friend said to me, "Why should you do it?" And we arranged it all. I sent a farewell letter, and on the following day they found on the shore my clothes, pocketbook and letters. I can't swim, you see.

PETUSHKOV: But how about the body? Didn't they ever find it?

FEDYA: They did; just imagine—a week later some sort of a body was found. My wife was called to identify it. The body was in a state of decay; she looked at it. "Is that he?" "Yes, it's he." And that ended it. I was buried, they were married, and are living here in prosperity. And I—well, here you see me! I live and drink. I passed by their house yesterday. The windows were lighted up, someone's shadow was thrown on one of the window shades. Sometimes I feel rather sad, but at other times it doesn't trouble me. I feel sad when I haven't any money—(*drinks.*)

ARTEMYEV: (*goes over*) You must excuse me, but I heard your story. It's a very good story, and especially a useful one. You say you feel badly when you have no money. Nothing can be worse than that. But you, in your position, should always have money. You're a corpse; you say. Very well——

FEDYA: Excuse me, but I didn't tell my story to you, and I don't want your advice.

ARTEMYEV: But I want to give it to you. You're a corpse; but suppose you should be resurrected, then what will they turn out to be, your wife and that gentleman, those two who are prospering? They will be bigamists, and in the best case will be asked to proceed to the less remote parts of Siberia. Then, why should you be short of money?

FEDYA: I ask you to leave me alone.

ARTEMYEV: All you have to do is to write a letter. If you want me to, I will write it for you; only give me their address, and you will thank me for it.

FEDYA: Go away! Was I talking to you? I didn't say anything to you.

ARTEMYEV: You certainly did. This man is a witness. The waiter also heard you say you were a corpse.

WAITER: I don't know anything about it, if you please.

FEDYA: (*to Artemyev*) Scoundrel!

ARTEMYEV: You call me a scoundrel? Police! Police! We'll have this recorded. (*Fedya rises to go out. Artemyev holds him back. A policeman appears.*)

TABLEAU II

The action takes place in the country, on a piazza overgrown with ivy.

SCENE I.

Anna Dmitrievna Karenina, Liza (pregnant), the nurse with the boy.

LIZA: By this time he is already leaving the station.

BOY: Who's coming?

LIZA: Papa.

BOY: Papa is leaving the station!

LIZA: C'est étonnant comme il l'aime, tout-à-fait comme son père.

ANNA DMITRIEVNA: Tant mieux. Se souvient-il de son père véritable?

LIZA: (*sighing*) I don't ever speak of him to the child. I always think, why should I confuse him? Then again I think that I ought to tell him. What do you think, mamma?

ANNA DMITRIEVNA: I think, Liza, that it depends just on how one feels about it, and if you will leave it to your feelings, your heart will tell you what you should say and when to say it. What a wonderful conciliator death is! I admit that there was once a time when Fedya—I knew him when he was a child, you know—was unwelcome to me, but now I only remember him as a lovely youth, a friend of Victor's, as that passionate person who, even though it was unlawful and irreligious, sacrificed himself for those he loved. On aura beau dire, l'action est belle—I hope Victor will not forget to bring home some yarn, I'm almost all out of it. (*continues knitting.*)

LIZA: I hear him coming.

(*The sound of wheels and bells is heard. Liza rises and goes to the end of the piazza.*)

LIZA: There's some one with him; a lady with a hat on. It's mamma! I haven't seen her for an age! (*goes to the door.*)

SCENE II.

Liza, Anna Dmitrievna, the nurse with the child. Karenin and Anna Pavlovna.

ANNA PAVLOVNA: (*embraces Liza and Anna Dmitrievna*) Victor met me and carried me off with him.

ANNA DMITRIEVNA: He certainly did well.

ANNA PAVLOVNA: Yes, of course. I thought to myself: when will I get a chance to see them? I always keep postponing my visit. So here I am to stay—if you will not drive me out—till the evening train.

VICTOR KARENIN: (*embraces his wife, his mother, and the child*) If you only knew how happy I am! You may congratulate me. I have two days' leave. To-morrow they will get along without me.

LIZA: Splendid! Two whole days! You haven't had that much for a long time. We'll take a ride down to the hermitage. Yes?

ANNA PAVLOVNA: What a resemblance! What a fine youngster! I only hope he will not inherit everything. His father's heart——

ANNA DMITRIEVNA: But not his weaknesses.

LIZA: Everything, everything! Victor agrees with me that if only he had been properly guided in his youth——

ANNA PAVLOVNA: Well, I don't understand anything of that. I simply can't think of him without tears.

LIZA: So it is with us. How his image has grown in our memory!

ANNA PAVLOVNA: Yes, I should say so.

LIZA: How hopeless it all seemed at one time. And how everything was solved all at once.

ANNA DMITRIEVNA: Well, Victor, did you bring me some yarn?

VICTOR KARENIN: I did, I did. (*goes to his bag and takes out several packages*) Here's your yarn, here is the cologne water, here are some letters, and here is an official envelope addressed to you. (*handing it to his wife*) Well, Anna Pavlovna, if you want to use the wash-room, I'll show you the way. I have to fix up a bit too, for dinner will be ready soon. Liza, I'll show Anna Pavlovna to the lower side-room, shall I not?

LIZA: (*pale, holds the letter with shivering hands, and reads.*)

VICTOR KARENIN: What is the matter with you, Liza, what is it?

LIZA: He's alive! My God! When will he at last set me free? Victor! What does it all mean? (*sobbing.*)

VICTOR KARENIN: (*takes the paper and reads*) This is terrible!

ANNA DMITRIEVNA: What is it? Speak!

VICTOR KARENIN: This is terrible. He is alive, she is a bigamist, and I am a criminal. This is a paper from the prosecuting attorney who demands Liza's presence in court.

ANNA DMITRIEVNA: What a wicked man! Why did he do it?

VICTOR KARENIN: It was all a lie, a lie!

LIZA: Oh, how I hate him! I don't know what I'm saying——(*leaves in tears. Karenin follows her.*)

SCENE III.

Anna Dmitrievna and Anna Pavlovna.

ANNA PAVLOVNA: How did he manage to remain alive?

ANNA DMITRIEVNA: I only know that the moment Victor came in contact with that world of filth, I said it would drag him down. And now it has happened. It's all deception, all lies!

ACT VI.

TABLEAU I

Office of the Prosecuting Attorney, who is sitting behind the table, conversing with Meljnikov. Near them the clerk is sorting papers.

SCENE I.

Prosecuting Attorney, Meljnikov, and the clerk.

PROSECUTING ATTORNEY: I never told her that. She made it all up, and now she blames me for it.

MELJNIKOV: She doesn't blame anyone, but she is grieving over it.

PROSECUTING ATTORNEY: Very well, then, I'll come for dinner. And now we come to a very interesting case. Show them in.

CLERK: Both of them?

PROSECUTING ATTORNEY: (*stops smoking and hides his cigarette*) No, only Madame Karenin or, to be more accurate, Madame Protasov, by her first husband's name.

MELJNIKOV: (*leaving*) Oh, it's that Madame Karenin.

PROSECUTING ATTORNEY: Yes. A nasty case. To be sure, I'm only beginning the investigation, but it looks bad. Well, good-bye. (*Meljnikov goes out.*)

SCENE II.

Prosecuting Attorney, clerk, and Lisa. (Enters heavily veiled, all in black.)

PROSECUTING ATTORNEY: Be seated, please. (*showing her to a chair*) Believe me, I very much regret the necessity of questioning you, but the conditions necessitate it— Please compose yourself, and know that you may refuse to answer certain of the questions, if you so desire. Only my opinion is that it's best for you, and for all concerned, to tell the truth. That's always better and more practical.

LIZA: I have nothing to conceal.

PROSECUTING ATTORNEY: (*looking at the paper*) Your name, station, and religion—that's all down here, isn't it?

LIZA: Yes.

PROSECUTING ATTORNEY: You are accused of having married another man, knowing that your husband was alive.

LIZA: I didn't know it.

PROSECUTING ATTORNEY: Also, of having persuaded your husband, by bribing him, to practice deception, to pretend to have committed suicide, with a view towards getting rid of him.

LIZA: All that is not true.

PROSECUTING ATTORNEY: Then permit me to ask you a few questions. Did you send him money, twelve hundred roubles, in July of last year?

LIZA: That money belonged to him. I procured it by selling his belongings. And during the period following our separation, when I was waiting for a divorce, I sent it to him.

PROSECUTING ATTORNEY: Very well. That money was sent on the 17th of July, two days before his disappearance?

LIZA: I think it was on the 17th of July; I don't remember.

PROSECUTING ATTORNEY: And when the police asked you to inspect the dead body, how was it that you identified it as your husband's?

LIZA: I was so excited at the time being that I didn't look at the body, and I was so sure that it was his, that when they asked me I answered: I think it's his.

PROSECUTING ATTORNEY: I see, you didn't examine it closely on account of your excitement, which we can well imagine. Very well. And now, permit me to ask you, why was money sent every month to Saratov, to the very city where your first husband was living?

LIZA: That money was sent by my husband, and I cannot tell you anything about its destination, since I knew nothing about it. Only it was not sent to Feodor Vasilyevich. We were perfectly sure that he no longer existed. That I can tell you definitely.

PROSECUTING ATTORNEY: Very well. Let me point out one thing to you: Madame—we are the servants of the Law, but that doesn't prevent us from being human. Believe me, therefore, that I fully understand your position and sympathize with you. You were tied down to a man who spent your fortune, betrayed you, in a word, caused unhappiness to——

LIZA: I loved him.

PROSECUTING ATTORNEY: Yes, but nevertheless, you had the natural desire to be free from him, and you chose this simple means, not realizing that it would lead to what is considered a crime—bigamy—I can understand that. And the judges too will understand it. Therefore, I should advise you to make a clean breast of it.

LIZA: But I have nothing to confess. I never lied. (*weeps*) Do you need me any longer?

PROSECUTING ATTORNEY: I should like to have you stay another while. I shall not trouble you any more with questions. Only read this, please, and sign it. Here's the cross-examination. Are your answers put down correctly? Right here, please. (*points to a chair at the window*) (*to the clerk*) Call Mr. Karenin.

SCENE III.

The prosecuting attorney, the clerk, Liza. Karenin enters. (seriously, solemnly.)

PROSECUTING ATTORNEY: Be seated, please.

VICTOR KARENIN: Thank you. (*remains standing*) What do you want?

PROSECUTING ATTORNEY: I am obliged to cross-examine you.

VICTOR KARENIN: In what capacity?

PROSECUTING ATTORNEY: (*smiling*) In my capacity of prosecuting attorney; and you are to be cross-examined in the capacity of defendant.

VICTOR KARENIN: How is that? With regard to what?

PROSECUTING ATTORNEY: With regard to having married a married woman. Permit me, however, to put the questions in the usual order. Be seated.

VICTOR KARENIN: Thank you.

PROSECUTING ATTORNEY: Your name?

VICTOR KARENIN: Victor Karenin.

PROSECUTING ATTORNEY: Station?

VICTOR KARENIN: Cavalier, councillor of state.

PROSECUTING ATTORNEY: Age?

VICTOR KARENIN: Thirty-eight years old.

PROSECUTING ATTORNEY: Faith?

VICTOR KARENIN: Greek-Orthodox. Never was tried or convicted before. Well?

PROSECUTING ATTORNEY: Did you know that Feodor Vasilyevich Protasov was alive when you married his wife?

VICTOR KARENIN: I did not know it. We were both convinced that he was drowned.

PROSECUTING ATTORNEY: To whom, then, were you sending money each month to Saratov, after the false reports of Protasov's death?

VICTOR KARENIN: I refuse to answer this question.

PROSECUTING ATTORNEY: Very well. What was your purpose in sending money, twelve hundred roubles, to Mr. Protasov, just before his alleged death, July 17?

VICTOR KARENIN: That money was given to me by my wife.

PROSECUTING ATTORNEY: By Mme. Protasov?

VICTOR KARENIN: —by my wife, to be sent to her husband. That money she considered his property and having broken off her connections with him, she considered it unfair to keep it.

PROSECUTING ATTORNEY: One more question, please. Why did you abandon your action for divorce?

VICTOR KARENIN: Because Feodor Vasilyevich took the matter upon himself and informed me of it in a letter.

PROSECUTING ATTORNEY: Have you that letter?

VICTOR KARENIN: The letter is lost.

Prosecuting Attorney: How strange that everything that might tend to convince the court of the validity of your testimony is either lost or absent.

Victor Karenin: Anything else you need?

Prosecuting Attorney: I don't need anything except to fulfil my duty, but you need to clear yourself, and I just advised Mme. Protasov and should advise you to do the same: not to hide what is self-evident and to tell everything, just as it happened, all the more so since Mr. Protasov is in such a state that he has already disclosed everything, and will, probably, testify to the same things before the court. I should advise——

Victor Karenin: I should like to ask you to confine yourself to the limits of your duties and refrain from giving us advice. May we go? (*approaches Liza. She rises and takes him by the hand.*)

Prosecuting Attorney: I am very sorry to have to detain you. (*Karenin turns around in surprise*) Oh, no, I don't mean that you are under arrest. Although it would have been better for the establishment of the truth, I shall not take recourse to that measure. I should only like to cross-examine Protasov in your presence and bring you face to face with him when you will have a better chance to contradict him. Please be seated. (*to the clerk*) Call Mr. Protasov.

SCENE IV.

The prosecuting attorney, the clerk, Liza, Karenin. Fedya enters, dirty and ragged.

Fedya: (*turning to Liza and Karenin*) Liza, Elizaveta Andreevna, Victor—It's not my fault. I meant to do better. And if it is my fault—forgive me, forgive me. (*bows very low before them.*)

PROSECUTING ATTORNEY: Please answer my questions.

FEDYA: Go ahead.

PROSECUTING ATTORNEY: Your name?

FEDYA: You know it.

PROSECUTING ATTORNEY: You'll please answer.

FEDYA: Well, Feodor Protasov.

PROSECUTING ATTORNEY: Your vocation, age, faith?

FEDYA: (*silent for a while*) Aren't you ashamed to ask these foolish questions? Ask what needs to be asked, and not such silly questions.

PROSECUTING ATTORNEY: I'll have to ask you to be more careful of what you say and to answer my questions.

FEDYA: Well, if you're not ashamed of it, then here you are: I am a bachelor of laws, forty years old, of the Greek-Orthodox faith; well, what else?

PROSECUTING ATTORNEY: Was it known to Mr. Karenin and your wife that you were alive when you left your clothes on the bank of the river and disappeared?

FEDYA: Certainly not. I really did want to kill myself, but then—well, never mind, that doesn't belong here. The point is that they knew nothing whatsoever about it.

PROSECUING ATTORNEY: How is it that you testified differently before the police-officer?

FEDYA: What police-officer? Ah, you mean when he came to me at the Rjanov House? I was drunk then and lied to him—I don't even remember what I said. But all that is nonsense. Now I'm not drunk and will tell the whole truth. They knew nothing. They believed I did not exist. And I was glad of it. And it would have remained that way, it not for that rascal Artemyev. If anyone is guilty it's no one but *I*.

PROSECUTING ATTORNEY: I understand your desire to be magnanimous, but the law demands the truth. Why was the money sent to you?

FEDYA: (*silent.*)

PROSECUTING ATTORNEY: Did you receive through Simonev the money that used to be sent to you to Saratov?

FEDYA: (*silent.*)

PROSECUTING ATTORNEY: Why don't you answer? It will go down on record that the defendant refused to answer these questions, which may do very much harm to you as well as to them. Well then?

FEDYA: (*silent; after a while*) Ah, sir, aren't you ashamed of yourself? Why are you intruding into other people's lives? You are glad you are in power, and in order to show it, you torture, mentally, if not physically, people who are a thousand times better than you are.

PROSECUTING ATTORNEY: I ask you——

FEDYA: You needn't take the trouble. I shall say all I have on my mind. (*to the clerk*) And you may take it down. At least there will for once be sensible human statements in your records. (*raising his voice*) Three people are living: I, he, and she. The relations between us are complicated—it's a struggle between good and evil, a spiritual struggle of which you have no conception. That struggle ends in a certain situation that solves everything. All are content. They are happy. They cherish my memory. I am happy in my downfall, at the thought of having done what was my duty—that I, a good-for-nothing, passed out of this life so as not to be in the way of those who are full of life and of goodness. And we are all living. Suddenly a scoundrel appears, a blackmailer, who demands that I should take a hand in a blackmailing scheme. I drive him away. He goes to you, the champions of justice, the guardians of morality. And you, receiving a few kopecks on the twentieth of each month for your nasty job, don your uniform, and with an easy conscience abuse these people, whose little finger is worth more than you are, who would not even let you step into their hall-way. But you have reached your aim and are glad——

PROSECUTING ATTORNEY: I shall have you led out of the room.

FEDYA: I am not afraid of anyone, for I'm a corpse, and you can do nothing with me: there is no position worse than my present one. Go ahead and tell them to lead me out.

VICTOR KARENIN: May we go?

PROSECUTING ATTORNEY: In a moment, after you will have signed the record.

FEDYA: How ridiculous you would be, if you were not so nasty!

PROSECUTING ATTORNEY: Lead him away. You are under arrest.

FEDYA: (*to Karenin and Liza*) I beg your forgiveness.

VICTOR KARENIN: (*goes over and shakes hands with him*) It evidently had to come to pass!

(*Liza passes by. Fedya bows low.*)

TABLEAU II.

A corridor of the district court-house. In the background is a glass door at which the sergeant-at-arms is stationed. Nearer to the right is another door through which the accused are led in. Ivan Petrovich Aleksandrov, in tatters, goes over to the first door and tries to pass through.

SCENE I

Sergeant-at-arms and Ivan Petrovich.

SERGEANT: Where are you going? No admittance here. Did you ever!

IVAN PETROVICH: Why not? The law says: the sessions are open to the public. (*applause within.*)

SERGEANT: No admittance here, that's all. I have strict orders.

IVAN PETROVICH: Boor! You don't know whom you are talking to. (*a young lawyer in a dress-suit comes out.*)

SCENE II.

Sergeant-at-arms, Ivan Petrovich and the young lawyer.

YOUNG LAWYER: What is it? Are you here on business?

IVAN PETROVICH: No, but I am the public. And this boor, this Cerberus, doesn't want to let me in.

YOUNG LAWYER: But this is not the place for the public.

IVAN PETROVICH: I know it, but I am different from anybody else.

YOUNG LAWYER: Wait; the intermission comes soon. (*turns to go; meets Prince Abrezkov.*)

SCENE III.

The sergeant-at-arms, Ivan Petrovich, the young lawyer and Prince Abrezkov.

PRINCE ABREZKOV: Permit me to inquire, how is the trial progressing?

YOUNG LAWYER: The lawyers are pleading—Petrushin is talking. (*more applause from within.*)

PRINCE ABREZKOV: How are the defendants bearing up?

YOUNG LAWYER: They display considerable self-control, especially Karenin and Elizaveta Andreevna. They make you feel that it is not they who are being judged, but that they are the ones who are judging society. That is the point that Petrushin is emphasizing.

PRINCE ABREZKOV: Well, and how is Protasov?

YOUNG LAWYER: Very much excited. He is trembling all over; but that was to be expected, after his manner of living. He is easily irritated; several times he interrupted the district attorney, as well as the lawyers. He's in a sorry state of exhaustion.

PRINCE ABREZKOV: What decision do you expect?

YOUNG LAWYER: It's hard to foresee. At any rate, they cannot prove premeditated action, but just the same—— (*a gentleman comes out. Prince Abrezkov moves towards the door*) Do you want to go in?

PRINCE ABREZKOV: Yes, I should like to.

YOUNG LAWYER: (*to the Sergeant-at-arms*) Admit this gentleman. There's a vacant seat right there on the left (*the Sergeant-at-arms admits Prince Abrezkov. As the door is opened, the lawyer can be seen pleading.*)

SCENE IV.

The Sergeant-at-arms, the young lawyer and Ivan Petrovich.

IVAN PETROVICH: Those aristrocats! I'm an aristocrat of the mind, which is more important.

YOUNG LAWYER: You'll excuse me. (*leaving.*)

SCENE V.

The Sergant-at-arms, Ivan Petrovich and Petushkov. (Petushkov comes hurrying in.)

PETUSHKOV: Ah, how do you do, Ivan Petrovich? How's the trial getting along?

IVAN PETROVICH: The lawyers are still talking. And they don't admit anyone, as you see.

SERGEANT: Stop your noise, there! This is not a bar-room!

(*More applause; the door opens. The lawyers and the spectators, both men and women, pass out.*)

SCENE VI.

The same; a lady and an officer.

LADY: Splendid! He actually made me cry.

OFFICER: It's better than any novel. Only it is inconceivable how she could have loved him so much. He's a terrible specimen.

SCENE VII.

The same. Another door opens. The defendants pass out and pass along the corridor; first Liza and Karenin, and behind them Fedya, alone.

LADY: Hush! Here he is! Just see how excited he is! (*The lady and the officer pass along.*)

FEDYA: (*going over to Ivan Petrovich.*) Did you bring it?

IVAN PETROVICH: Here it is. (*handing him something.*)

FEDYA: (*hides it in his pocket and is about to go; notices Petushkov*) It's stupid, silly! And tedious. Nonsensical. (*is about to go.*)

SCENE VIII.

The same; Petrushin, the principal lawyer, stout, red-faced, lively, approaches.

PETRUSHIN: Well, my friend, we have a good chance, only don't spoil it all in your final plea.

FEDYA: I won't say a word. What shall I tell them? I won't do it.

PETRUSHIN: No, you must! Don't let yourself get excited. Now, we have as good as won the case. You have only to tell them what you told me, that if you are on trial, it's only for not having committed suicide,—that is, for not having done what is considered a sin by the church and a crime by the law.

FEDYA: I won't say a single word.

PETRUSHIN: Why not?

FEDYA: I simply don't want to, and I'm not going to. Just tell me this: what is the worst than can happen?

PETRUSHIN: I have told you already: in the worst case it may mean exile to Siberia.

FEDYA: Who do you mean will be exiled?

PETRUSHIN: Why, both you and your wife.

FEDYA: And in the best case?

PETRUSHIN: Religious penance, and, of course, annihilation of the second marriage.

FEDYA: That means that they will again tie us together.

PETRUSHIN: Why, yes, as a matter of course. But don't let that excite you. And please do just as I tell you, and, above all, don't say anything unnecessary. However— (*noticing that people have gathered about them and are listening*) I am tired, I will take a bit of rest. The main thing is—courage.

FEDYA: And there can be no other solution?

PETRUSHIN: (*going away*) None whatever.

SCENE IX.

The same, without Petrushin; a court attendant enters.

ATTENDANT: Move along! Move along! Don't stand in the corridor!

FEDYA: Just a minute. (*takes the pistol out of his pocket and shoots himself straight in the heart. He falls. All rush towards him.*) Never mind. I think it's all right. Liza!——

SCENE X.

From all sides spectators rush in, also judges, defendants and witnesses. First of all comes Liza. Behind her are Masha, Karenin, Ivan Petrovich and Prince Abrezkov.

LIZA: What have you done! Fedya! Why——!

FEDYA: Forgive me for not having been able—to liberate you otherwise— It's not for your sake—it's much better for me. I've been ready for it—for a long time.

LIZA: You will live. (*The doctor bends over him, listening.*)

FEDYA: I know without the doctor—— Victor, good-bye. And Masha—came too late—(*weeping*) How well I feel, how well—(*expires.*)

(*Curtain.*)

FROM THE LIST

OF

NICHOLAS L. BROWN

CPSIA information can be obtained
at www.ICGtesting.com
Printed in the USA
LVOW03s0235060616
491359LV00025B/801/P

9 781276 49